THE MINDFUL EATING WORKBOOK

THE MINDFUL EATING WORKBOOK

Simple Mindfulness Practices to Nurture
a Healthy Relationship with Food

VINCCI TSUI, RD

ALTHEA
PRESS

Editor: Nana K. Twumasi
Production Editor: Erum Khan

Author photo © f8 Photography Inc.

ISBN: Print 978-1-64152-314-1
eBook 978-1-64152-315-8

R1

To you, the reader:
It is my sincere hope that you find wisdom, self-discovery,
and inner strength that move you toward a more fulfilling future.

CONTENTS

INTRODUCTION

What Exactly Is Mindful Eating?

When I ask some of the groups I teach what they think "mindful eating" means, I tend to get a variety of answers, such as, "I'm mindful about what I put into my body," and, "It's about slowing down and savoring every bite," and, "Mindful eating forces you to eat slower, so that you get fuller faster." Sadly, these answers capture some of the many misconceptions about mindful eating.

Mindful eating is not about eating better, getting healthier, or losing weight. So why am I, as a dietitian, even talking about it? Mindful eating does something more powerful: It changes your relationship with food and with your body. As you bring the concepts of mindful eating into the rest of your life, you may also find that it changes the way you engage with the world.

> [Mindful eating] changes your relationship with food and with your body . . . it changes the way you engage with the world.

When I first learned about mindful eating, it took a while for me to accept this approach and integrate it into my own life; I wasn't sure I needed it. I thought it was too "spiritual," and even though I ate with distractions most of the time and didn't give much thought to my eating habits, I was happy with my food choices and in good health.

What eventually led me to experience the benefits of mindfulness and integrate some of the concepts into my work and life was practicing yoga. Like most people, I initially viewed it as a gentler, more approachable physical activity. However, I've been fortunate to have instructors who have infused yoga philosophy into their classes, encouraging students to trust their bodies and intuition. It's the one activity where I actually believe it when the instructor says that I can move however I'd like, regardless of their cues. Coupled with some of the other learning I've done in regard to mindful eating and related approaches, it's now apparent to me that the way I interact with food and eating is different from how it was before.

With this workbook, I want to help cut through the noise around mindful eating and share some of the core concepts and related philosophies that have changed my work as a dietitian, as well as how I behave in my personal life. This workbook presents some of these ideas in an interactive way, so that it'll be easier for you to try them and perhaps incorporate them into your own daily habits.

The discussions and exercises in this workbook will help you practice eating mindfully, but this is only the beginning. I encourage you to seek out the support you need to continue to build your practice. You may want to read this book and complete the exercises under the guidance of a dietitian, therapist, or other health professional that specializes in mindful eating and/or mindfulness, if possible. My own learning has involved reading many books and articles, attending webinars and workshops, participating in online groups, listening to podcasts, and growing my yoga practice. My hope is that the knowledge I share with you in this workbook solidifies your desire to begin a mindful eating practice.

CHAPTER ONE

THE MINDFUL PATH

This chapter lays the groundwork for building your mindful eating practice. You will learn about the benefits of mindfulness and mindful eating, as well as practical strategies for habit change. We'll end the chapter with a taste of mindful eating to whet your appetite for the activities ahead.

What Is Mindfulness?

Jon Kabat-Zinn, who is often referred to as the father of mindfulness, defines "mindfulness" as "awareness that arises through paying attention, on purpose, in the present moment, non-judgmentally."

Though the concept of mindfulness has a centuries-long history within Buddhism, Kabat-Zinn is credited with bringing mindfulness into modern, mainstream culture and presenting it from a scientific perspective, rather than a religious one. He created the Mindfulness-Based Stress Reduction (MBSR) program and what is now the Center for Mindfulness in Medicine, Health Care, and Society at UMass Medical School. In the four decades since Kabat-Zinn introduced MBSR, research has uncovered many benefits of a regular mindfulness practice.

LIVE WITH LESS STRESS

Slowing down and reducing stress are often the first benefits people think of when it comes to mindfulness practice and meditation. Despite its name, Kabat-Zinn's MBSR program was originally created to help people manage chronic pain. Still, a 2015 meta-analysis of research on the program found that MBSR can be effective at reducing stress, depression, anxiety, and distress, as well as improving the quality of life in healthy people. Research on other programs and on different populations has produced similar results.

GAIN SELF-AWARENESS

In Buddhist tradition, mindfulness meditation is used to help practitioners gain self-awareness and wisdom with the ultimate goal of achieving enlightenment—a state of perfect compassion, wisdom, and power attained through an awakening to all the qualities of the mind.

Many of us have a tendency to "live in our head," allowing ourselves to be consumed and defined by our thoughts and emotions. Because mindfulness is about being fully aware in the present moment, we attune not just to what's happening in our mind and our surroundings, but also to the physical sensations from within our body, a concept called *interoceptive awareness.*

A 2015 study in Germany found that after three months of daily mindfulness meditation practice, subjects reported improved interoceptive awareness in five areas—attention regulation, emotional awareness, self-regulation, body listening, and trusting—compared to people who didn't have a regular meditation practice.

Attuning to your body's cues can help you become more aware of your physical and mental needs, giving you more knowledge and tools to take the steps to meet those needs and practice better self-care.

IMPROVE MEMORY

Studies have shown that mindfulness practice can improve short- and long-term memory. In a 2016 study published in PLOS One, researchers found that even listening to a short guided meditation resulted in better performance on a memory test.

Furthermore, research on mindfulness interventions in people with dementia has been promising. Though there is only a handful of studies on this topic, there is a trend in the available research toward reduction in cognitive decline and increase in quality of life, along with other benefits, for practicing mindfulness.

BOOST MOOD

Research consistently shows that mindfulness is associated with feelings of happiness and well-being. In one study, 400 healthcare workers were asked to complete questionnaires on their level of happiness, self-compassion, mindfulness, life conditions, and habits. It was found that higher levels of self-compassion and mindfulness were associated with higher levels of happiness.

A similar survey of 140 student-athletes found that happiness was more related to internal factors, like mindfulness, self-efficacy, self-restraint, and self-esteem, rather than external factors like athletic or academic achievements.

Regular mindfulness practice can increase happiness, even after a short time. A 2015 study that followed a group of women for three weeks found that those who kept a mindfulness diary and did a mindfulness meditation four times a week reported less depression and stress, and more happiness, compared to women who didn't do any mindfulness exercises.

GET FOCUSED

Mindfulness practice can also help improve concentration and focus. Surprisingly, there isn't a lot of available research on this topic, though the results of the existing research are promising. For example, a 2014 study published in *Psychotherapy Research* found that mindfulness training improved attention and focus in psychology students. Similarly, a 2013 study found that mindfulness training can reduce distracting thoughts and "mind wandering."

In my own work, I've found that mindfulness has helped me be more present when working with clients so that I can better attend to their needs.

> "Life is so brief that we should not glance either too far backwards or forwards . . . therefore study how to fix our happiness in our glass and in our plate."
> —*Grimod de la Reynière*

Why Eat Mindfully?

While the most traditional way of practicing mindfulness is meditation, it is possible to incorporate mindfulness into other activities. It might be checking in with yourself at random moments during the day and noticing, without judgment, how you feel. It might be paying attention to what all your senses are taking in during an otherwise routine task, like driving to work or getting the mail.

Mindful eating brings the concepts of mindfulness to the experience of eating. The Center for Mindful Eating describes mindful eating as using all of our senses to be present in the entire eating experience, including choosing and preparing the food, while acknowledging our inner wisdom and body cues without judgment.

In addition to the benefits of mindfulness itself, mindful eating has several of its own benefits.

ENJOY YOUR FOOD

In our fast-paced, on-the-move society, eating often feels automatic. It's not uncommon for us to forget what we ate the day before, let alone how it tasted. I suggested earlier that mindful eating isn't about slowing down and savoring our food, but it is a good way to introduce the idea of being present and using all our senses to take in the eating experience.

When we actually take the time to taste our food, the results can be surprising. In a 2014 study published in *Mindfulness* journal, subjects were more likely to rank foods that are typically not enjoyed—specifically, anchovies, wasabi peas, and prunes—more enjoyable after a mindful eating exercise compared to those who ate the same foods without applying mindfulness strategies.

MORE SATISFYING MEALTIMES

Another thing that's missing for a lot of people is the experience of truly satisfying mealtimes. If we're just rushing through our day, barely tasting our food, how can we feel satisfied?

A satisfying meal doesn't need to be a sit-down dinner with candles, soft music, and fancy china. Even if you're sitting at your desk, eating something you don't particularly enjoy, mindful eating is an opportunity to be present and observe the situation without judgment and perhaps create the space for you to ask yourself what you can do to make mealtime more satisfying.

Sometimes it's something that you can do right away, like putting away your phone or moving away from any distractions. Other times it's something you might make note of for later, like a tweak to your recipe, or perhaps remembering to have a treat for dessert. We need to eat to survive, so why not make it something we enjoy?

BETTER HEALTH OUTCOMES

For some, the thought of joy and pleasure in eating is seen as a bad or negative thing. You may have heard the saying, "If something tastes good, it can't be good for us." Good news: When it comes to mindful eating, you *can* have your cake and eat it—nay, enjoy it!—too.

Research has shown that mindful eating is correlated with decreased emotional eating, binge eating, depression, anxiety, and emotional stress. It is also correlated with healthier food choices and improved blood-sugar control, relationship to food, and body image. Mindful eating interventions have been investigated in a variety of patient populations, including disordered eating and type-2 diabetes.

EXERCISE: PAINTED PICTURE

Although the focus of mindful eating is on the present moment, sometimes it is helpful to look ahead to the future to provide some guidance on where we would like to go with our practice. Reflect on what made you decide to read this workbook using the following prompts and write your responses in the space provided:

- What are you hoping to learn?
- What would your life be like when you have a regular mindful eating practice? In other words, what would you see, do, have, and be?
- "Paint a picture" by describing a typical day in your future life with a regular mindful eating practice.

What Mindful Practice Involves

You don't need incense or meditation beads to practice mindfulness and mindful eating. The practices have come a long way from their religious roots. Mindfulness and mindful eating are simply about engaging in the world in a different way. I've summarized my practice into the following four principles, which we will revisit throughout this workbook.

VINCCI'S FOUR MINDFULNESS PRACTICE PRINCIPLES

1. **Press Pause and Be Present:** Most of us live our lives at breakneck speed, always thinking of the next step and wearing "busy" like a badge of honor. Mindfulness is an invitation for you to switch gears, temporarily let go of thinking about the past or the future, and focus on the present moment.

   You might find it helpful to create a small ritual, like moving to a specific location or taking a few deep, cleansing breaths, as a way to signal to yourself to begin your practice.

   During the practice, it's normal to notice your mind wandering off to another thought throughout the practice. Simply "press pause" and bring yourself to the present again.

2. **Curiosity, Not Judgment:** As we go through life, we bring with us our years of lived experience and education. This serves us by making our lives richer and more efficient—if we had to learn everything all over again every day, we wouldn't get anything done!

   In the context of mindfulness and mindful eating, our personal catalog of experiences can hold us back. For example, we might be so used to eating in a certain way that it can be hard to change, or perhaps we're used to eating some foods so much that we don't think to take the time to really taste and enjoy them. I invite you to enter the situation as though you were a child, alien, or scientist (or child alien scientist!). The new perspective may help you let go of your preconceived notions and be present in the situation.

3. **Sensing, Not Slowing:** When I first learned about mindful eating, I was taught to set a timer for 20 to 30 minutes and try to stretch my meal to last that time, or put my fork down between bites to slow my eating. This might

MINDFUL EATING AND WEIGHT

Sometimes people come to mindful eating with the goal of weight loss. Arguably, this is an outcome of what is termed *diet culture*, which describes the way our culture upholds thinness as a beauty ideal and encourages the pursuit of weight loss as a way to gain health and moral value. Indeed, there are many weight-management programs that teach mindful eating, and many studies show that mindful eating is correlated with lower body weight.

My position, which reflects that of The Center for Mindful Eating, is that mindful eating is not for weight loss. While it's absolutely possible to lose weight when you eat mindfully, it's also possible for your weight to stay the same or go up. There are numerous factors that contribute to a person's weight, many of which we cannot control.

More important, mindful eating is about being in the present moment. If we are focusing on a future outcome, like eating less or losing weight, it distracts us from being truly present. It can also be difficult to remain nonjudgmental if mindful eating is not producing the outcome we want.

be a helpful introduction for some, but what's the point of slowing down if you don't know why you're doing it?

In mindfulness practice, the purpose of slowing down is so that you can use your senses to experience each moment. What do you see, hear, smell, taste, and feel in your environment and in your body? Allow yourself to cycle through each sense from moment to moment. Over time, you might find that you don't need to slow down to get the information you need.

Contrary to popular belief, the goal of mindfulness is *not* to think or feel nothing. It's normal for thoughts and emotions to come up during this time. Similar to what you're experiencing with your senses, simply notice any thoughts or emotions that may arise, and allow them to move on as you redirect your attention back to your senses. The practice lies in bringing yourself back to the present.

4. **Practice, Not Perfection:** I'm careful to avoid the phrase "mindful eater," nor do I describe mindful eating as a "journey." Not only is the latter cheesy, but it also implies there is a final destination. Mindfulness and mindful eating are ongoing practices, and you will never stop learning and building on your knowledge and habits. It's when we think we have all the answers that we get ourselves into trouble.

    Don't feel discouraged if you feel as though you're not "getting it right." Mindful eating is not like a diet where there are set rules, restrictions, and a clear definition of "right" and "wrong." Instead, you'll be trying to undo lots of ingrained habits and beliefs that are often reinforced by society. Have patience and trust that you are doing important, worthwhile work.

EXERCISE: MINDFUL EATING ASSESSMENT

This assessment is adapted from the 20-Item Italian Mindful Eating Questionnaire created by psychologist and The Center for Mindful Eating board member Dr. Cecilia Clementi and colleagues. The original questionnaire assesses for **awareness** of how food affects how you feel and for **recognition** of hunger and fullness cues. This assessment includes additional questions concerning **nonjudgment**.

Answer yes or no for each statement. In some cases, you might feel you fall somewhere in the middle. If that's the case, read over the statement a few times, and answer according to how you would *usually* act most of the time.

Awareness

1. Before I eat, I take a moment to appreciate colors and smells of food.   Y   N

2. I notice when the food I eat affects my emotional state.   Y   N

3. I taste every bite of food I eat.   Y   N

4. I recognize when I am eating and not hungry.   Y   N

Recognition of Hunger/Fullness

5. I stop eating when I am full, even when it is something I love.   Y   N

6. I recognize when I feel hungry, as opposed to other sensations, like thirsty or bored.   Y   N

7. If there is extra food I like, I take a second helping even though
   I am full.   Y   N

8. I only allow myself to eat at set mealtimes and snack times,
   regardless of how I feel.   Y   N

Nonjudgment

9. I categorize foods into "good" or "bad," based on how healthy
   I think they are.   Y   N

10. I don't allow myself to eat certain foods (aside from allergens). Y   N

11. I get upset with myself if I eat something unhealthy or if I eat too much. Y   N

12. I strive to be a "perfect eater."   Y   N

SCORING

For questions 1 to 6, give yourself 1 point for every "yes." For questions 7 to 12, give yourself 1 point for every "no." Then tally up your points for each of the three sections and record them here:

Category	Score
Awareness	
Recognition of Hunger/Fullness	
Nonjudgment	
Total Score	

The highest total score is 12 with 4 points in each category. High scores in each category and overall indicate better mindful eating skills. Keep in mind that there are many people who practice mindful eating regularly and do not have a "perfect" score.

This assessment is for interest only, so it is not meant to diagnose anything. Instead, it provides you with awareness of where you are now with your mindful eating. You may choose to complete this assessment again after you finish this workbook to help you track your progress.

MINDFULNESS AND MEDITATION: BEST PRACTICES

Though meditation is not necessary for mindful eating, it is often recommended to help you build your mindfulness practice and bring it into other areas of your life. If you are new to meditation, here are some tips to help you get started.

Find a Meditation Spot. Choose a location where you can sit or lie down comfortably, undisturbed. You might choose to sit on the ground, or you may feel more comfortable in a chair or on a cushion. Candles, incense, and crystals are nice but are certainly not mandatory. Your meditation spot doesn't have to be glamorous—I have even meditated in closets!

Start Small. Meditation doesn't have to take a lot of time—you might set a timer for one minute or decide to meditate for 5 to 10 slow breaths. As you become more familiar and comfortable with meditating, you may choose to meditate for longer periods.

Anchor Your Thoughts. Contrary to popular belief, meditation is not about emptying your mind; rather, it's about focusing your attention on the present moment. Often, the breath is used as an anchor, as each breath is unique to each moment. Others might choose music or a mantra. A guided meditation can also be helpful; they can be easily found online, and there are many apps, such as Insight Timer, Headspace, or Calm, that have meditations for beginners.

Practice, Not Perfection. Many people say that they aren't good at meditation because their mind always wanders, or they get bored or distracted. The practice of meditation lies in bringing yourself back to the present moment; whenever you notice yourself getting lost in thought or even scratching an itch, as long as you are gently reminding yourself to return to the present, you are meditating.

Why We Eat

A colleague of mine once said, "Saying food is only for fuel is like saying sex is only for procreation." Though the primary reason we eat is to get energy and nutrients, food is so much more.

Most of us have the privilege to be in a position where food is easily accessible, plentiful, clean, and safe. We have a seemingly endless array of flavors and textures to choose from, with about 20,000 new foods introduced to the market annually. Nutrition and health battle with taste, convenience, cost, and other factors when it comes to how we decide what to eat. But why exactly do we eat? Let's take a look.

WE EAT TO FUEL

Most foods are a complex blend of energy, water, fiber, vitamins, minerals, antioxidants, and/or other compounds. In diet culture, however, food is seen as nothing more than "calories in, calories out" and eating has become a numbers game: You are "good" if you eat fewer calories and lose weight, and you are "bad" if you eat more calories and gain weight.

This attitude of "calories in, calories out" is an oversimplification of eating, weight, and health. Genetics, medical status, medications, hormones, stress, and sleep are just some of the many factors that can affect weight. Weight is also a poor indicator of a person's health status or eating habits—living in a larger body doesn't mean that a person is unhealthy or has poor eating habits, while living in a smaller body doesn't mean that a person is healthy or has good eating habits.

Reducing food to a calorie count ignores the fact that it gives us energy to move and think, as well as nutrients to support our health. Food keeps our heart beating, our lungs breathing, and our body strong and functioning. Food is more than something that might affect our weight. We need food to survive.

WE EAT TO SATISFY

In my practice, I see people who carry a lot of shame for having cravings and/or eating for pleasure. Diet culture has taught us that it's wrong to eat if we don't need to, as it could lead to weight gain. Again, our weight is not a reflection of how and why we eat, nor is food simply a source of fuel and calories. There is nothing wrong with wanting to eat, or having a craving, even if it's not something our body "needs."

Evolutionary scientists believe we gain pleasure from food as a survival mechanism. If food was not pleasurable, our prehistoric ancestors would not have been driven to seek it out, and we would not have survived as a species. These mechanisms also explain why certain foods and flavors are more pleasurable than others: Sweetness indicated that a fruit was ripe and safe to eat, while high-fat food served as a concentrated source of energy. In contrast, bitter plants were often poisonous.

Moreover, food is social. Our prehistoric ancestors probably ate together to maximize resources—it's much more efficient to build one big fire versus several small ones, and it probably took many people to eat the meat from a large animal before it spoiled. Nowadays, we continue to connect with others through food, whether it's sitting down for a family meal, celebrating a holiday or special event, or experiencing a different culture without having to travel. Pleasure and connection are just as important as nutrients when it comes to our health and well-being.

WE EAT TO SOOTHE

Like cravings, there is often a lot of guilt and shame around emotional eating. Again, it goes back to the narrative that "food is only for fuel." The stereotypical image of a girl crying over a tub of ice cream with a rom-com playing in the background probably doesn't help.

All eating can give us a hit of dopamine and endorphins—"feel good" chemicals in our brain and nervous system that can instantly lift our mood. Combined with the fact that food is quick and readily available to most, it's no wonder we turn to it for comfort. Emotional eating is normal and relatively benign when you consider some of the other possible coping mechanisms.

Emotional eating can become problematic, however, if it is keeping you from actually addressing the issue at hand or if it is your *only* coping mechanism. You'll have an opportunity to learn more about emotional eating in chapter 3 (see page 49).

WE EAT TO DISTRACT

Many of us turn to food when we're bored. We eat while sitting in front of the TV so that we can do something with our hands, or we catch ourselves nibbling on something "just because it's there." In a way, boredom eating is really just a form of emotional eating, but instead of soothing stronger feelings like sadness, anger, or stress, the emotion in this situation is the discomfort of not doing anything.

Living in a culture that values efficiency and productivity, it makes sense to feel like something is missing when we are not busy and on the go. It's natural that we would want to turn to food in these situations. It keeps us feeling busy without requiring a lot of effort. Like emotional eating, boredom eating is healthy and normal, though it can become problematic if you don't have any other coping skills in your toolbox. I'll share more about boredom eating in chapter 3 (page 49).

EXERCISE: THE LAST TIME YOU ATE

Use the following prompts to help you reflect on the last time you ate and write your responses in the space provided:

- When and where was the last time you ate?
- What made you decide to eat?
- What did you eat? (Describe it using all your senses: sight, smell, hearing, taste, and touch.)
- What thoughts and emotions came up as you were eating?
- What else was happening while you were eating (i.e., conversation, watching TV, reading, working, etc.)?
- How did you decide when to stop eating?
- What thoughts and emotions came up when you were finished eating?

....

....

....

....

....

....

....

....

....

....

You'll have an opportunity to do this exercise again in each of the upcoming chapters, using what you've learned to reflect on your mindful eating practice as it continues to develop.

Changing Our Habits

When you consider the way many of us eat today—hurriedly, while scrolling through social media on our phone or sitting in front of the TV—transitioning to eating mindfully could really mean breaking habits that have been established for years.

TIME TO EAT

One of the common misconceptions around using mindful eating to attune to our body cues is that the ultimate goal is to only eat according to our hunger and fullness cues. While this may be true in an ideal world, our hectic, heavily scheduled lives don't always allow for this.

We might eat preemptively, knowing that there might not be food available when we actually feel hungry, or we might eat to accommodate another person's needs. Certain medical conditions can also make our hunger and fullness signals unreliable. Use mindful eating as a tool to help you explore why you are eating at the times you do: Is it because you actually feel hungry or just because it is "time to eat"? Either way, there is no right or wrong answer.

So far, you've learned some of the benefits of mindfulness and mindful eating, and you've identified some of the mindful eating habits you are already practicing, plus some that might need more work. The difficulty is knowledge doesn't always equal action. I see many people in my practice who tell me, "I know what I need to do; I just need to do it." Changing your habits requires more than sheer willpower, but you *can* do it.

NEUROPLASTICITY

You may not be able to teach an old dog new tricks, but humans can learn and establish new habits throughout life. The ability for our brain to change over time is called neuroplasticity. When we form a habit, neurons in our brain form connections, creating a neural pathway. The more a habit is ingrained, the stronger the bond. When you are breaking a habit, you are literally trying to break a neural connection.

We can harness neuroplasticity research to help us learn how to break our old habits and replace them with newer ones. Research shows that all habits have a trigger, so the first step is to identify the cues, situations, emotions, or events that may be triggering your current habits. Once you have identified your triggers, the next step is responding to them differently, allowing your brain to establish a new neural pathway.

Mindfulness and meditation can increase neuroplasticity. Multiple studies have shown that mindfulness training and practice can cause positive changes in brain activity, including an increase in gray matter, the parts of our brain that are responsible for muscle control and sensory perception.

STAYING IN THE PRESENT

One of the main principles of mindfulness and mindful eating is being present. But staying in the present can be difficult when you consider how much time we spend thinking about the past (e.g., reminiscing, reflecting) or the future (e.g., making plans, setting goals, meeting deadlines).

When it comes to creating or changing habits, the conversation often centers on what we want to do or who we want to become. Shifting your focus to the present takes the pressure off this unknown future and focuses on the here and now: What do you need *now*? What are you doing *now* to try to meet your needs? This can help decrease overwhelming thoughts and move you toward the small actions necessary to snowball into bigger change. Of course, that doesn't mean you can't review your past and plan for the future to get the ball rolling, as you'll be doing in the next exercise.

EXERCISE: STEP-BY-STEP GUIDE TO HABIT CHANGE

This guide can help you create a game plan to change or stop an existing habit that is no longer serving you. Though this book focuses on changing habits that may be keeping you from eating mindfully or building a mindfulness practice, you can use these steps for any habit you are trying to stop or change, like biting your fingernails or going to bed late. Note that the steps don't always happen in this order, and you might find yourself returning to certain steps throughout the process.

1. **Identify what needs changing.** If you already have a clear idea of a habit that you would like to focus on, skip this step. Otherwise, let's kick things off with a **brain dump**. Set a timer for 10 minutes and write down everything you *could* change. If the timer goes off and the page isn't filled, set it for another 5 minutes and keep going.

2. **Get to know your habit.** From your brain dump, choose one habit you would like to focus on changing or stopping.

....

3. **Describe this habit in more detail.** What are its triggers? Does this habit tend to happen at certain times? Does this habit show up differently in different situations? You may want to answer this question from memory or pay attention to this habit for a few days and jot down your observations.

....

....

....

....

4. **Create new habits.** Reflect back on the "Painted Picture" exercise on page 6. How will changing this habit move you toward your painted picture, if at all? What will it look like when you successfully change this habit? What will you see, do, have, and be?

....

....

....

....

5. What are some action steps you can take to move you toward your "Painted Picture"?

....

....

....

....

....

....

Review the action steps you just listed, and choose some you would like to try the next time you notice a trigger. Write them in the space below.

As you work through this process, remember to have compassion for yourself. This habit did not happen overnight, so it's unrealistic to expect it to go away quickly. Have patience and allow the time to address your habit.

OBSERVATION LOG

Using this worksheet, keep a log of your progress in changing or stopping your habit. The first row has been completed as an example.

Date	Trigger (Describe the situation, thoughts, and emotions.)	Response	Notes (What went well? What might you do differently next time?)
January 13	Working overtime to meet a deadline. Feeling stressed, rushing so I could get home.	Noticed feeling of anxiety. Grabbed a chocolate bar.	Felt guilty at first for having chocolate, so I "pressed pause" and tried to enjoy the chocolate mindfully. It tasted really good! Noticed that having that short break was helpful. I wonder if the break would be as effective if there was no chocolate.

What to Look Forward To

Now that you've laid down some of the groundwork to develop your mindful eating practice, here is what to expect in the chapters ahead. The concepts in each chapter build upon one another, so although the information and exercises can stand on their own, it will make the most sense to go through this workbook sequentially.

Of course, if you get stuck on a certain exercise or if a certain section simply doesn't resonate with you, you can skip ahead and perhaps come back to it later. Trust your intuition to guide you when it comes to figuring out what will help you get the most out of this book.

CHAPTER TWO: IN YOUR BODY

Interoceptive awareness and embodiment are two key components of mindfulness and mindful eating. This chapter discusses strategies to effectively attune to your body's cues and how to interpret them so that you can better meet your body's needs. It also touches on how self-acceptance and gratitude can enhance your mindful eating practice.

CHAPTER THREE: IN YOUR BRAIN

It would be remiss to talk about mindful eating without talking about the mind. This chapter explores how our thoughts and emotions can impact our eating habits and how we can change some of those patterns and behaviors through mindful eating.

CHAPTER FOUR: AT THE TABLE

Here, we get into the nuts and bolts of mindful eating, and you'll have the opportunity to practice having a mindful meal from start to finish. This chapter also discusses how nutrition and health concerns fit in with your mindful eating practice.

CHAPTER FIVE: THE MINDFUL LIFESTYLE

This workbook concludes by extending your mindfulness practice beyond the dinner table and into daily life, including how to help your family and friends understand your practice and perhaps start their own.

> "The healing is in the return, not in never having left."
> —Sharon Salzberg

EXERCISE: A TASTE OF MINDFUL EATING

Let's close this chapter with a basic mindful eating exercise. Traditionally, this exercise is done with a raisin, but you may choose to do this activity with any finger food. You may want to record yourself reading the following passage, allowing enough time to follow the instructions as you read, and then play it back so that you can stay present in the activity.

Begin by placing the food in front of you, and settle comfortably in your seat. If you are sitting in a chair, place your feet flat on the ground. If you feel comfortable doing so, close your eyes. Take a few deep breaths, feeling the rise of your chest with each inhale and the fall with each exhale. Continue like this until you feel relaxed and grounded.

Open your eyes and look at the food in front of you. Approach the food with curiosity, as though you've never seen anything like it before. Notice the information your sense of sight is telling you about this food: its color, shape, size, and texture. Continue like this, without judgment.

Let's add the sense of touch. Pick up the food and notice how it feels in your hand. You may roll it between your fingers or place it in one hand, then the other. Notice what your sense of touch is telling you about this food—its texture, shape, and temperature. You may notice that your eyes are receiving new information as well. Continue like this, without judgment.

Hold the food up to your nose and inhale deeply. Notice what your sense of smell is telling you about this food. The sense of taste is closely linked to the sense of smell. Can you guess what this food might taste like based on how it smells? Continue like this, without judgment.

Now, take a bite of the food, or if it's small enough, place it in your mouth. Without chewing, roll it around with your tongue for a few moments. Notice what your senses of taste, touch, and smell are telling you about this food.

As you slowly begin to chew your food, notice what the sense of hearing is telling you about this food. Notice any new information that is being received by your senses of taste, touch, and smell, if at all. Continue like this, without judgment, as you chew and swallow your food in your own time.

REFLECTION

What was it like to taste your food this way? How does this compare to the way you normally eat?

....

....

....

....

....

....

....

Based on this exercise, what are some changes you might make to your current eating habits to help you eat more mindfully?

....

....

....

....

....

Chapter Check-in

In this chapter, you learned about mindfulness, mindful eating, and some of their benefits; the ins and outs of habit change to unlearn some current habits; and how to make space to establish your mindful eating practice.

What are some of your aha moments from this chapter? What are some areas you'd like to focus on as you continue to learn and build your practice?

....

....

....

....

....

....

....

CHAPTER TWO

IN YOUR BODY

If I had the opportunity to come up with a new name for "mindful eating," I would probably call it "embodied eating." Embodiment is the representation or expression of a quality or idea in physical form. Because mindfulness is not tangible, any act that is about being present in your body, such as mindful eating, can be a way to turn mindfulness into a physical practice.

It's interesting that we never question when we need to go to the restroom or when we're sleepy, yet when it comes to hunger, we'll do everything but acknowledge that we need to eat:

"But I just ate."

"I'm probably just confusing hunger with thirst. Let me have a glass of water and see how I feel."

"Maybe I'm just bored."

In this chapter, you'll practice embodying mindfulness through mindful eating by building your interoceptive awareness—specifically, attuning to your hunger and fullness cues. I'll also touch on some topics that I'm passionate about—the non-diet/anti-diet approach and self-compassion—and how these concepts relate to mindfulness and mindful eating. Let's begin with a basic body scan, a type of mindfulness meditation.

EXERCISE: BASIC BODY SCAN

This mindfulness meditation is popular with beginners, as it scans through the different parts of your body, allowing you to continue to shift your focus throughout, instead of focusing on one thing for an extended period of time.

For this meditation, you will be scanning up the right side of the body, then down the left, spending the length of one or two breaths on each part of the body. You may find that you have a different sequence and/or pace that works better for you. As you reach the different parts of your body, resist the urge to lessen, change, or get rid of the sensations you may feel, and instead, just notice.

You may want to record yourself reading the following passage, allowing enough time to follow the instructions as you read, and then play it back so that you can stay present in the activity.

Sit or lie down for this meditation, whichever feels most comfortable. If you are sitting in a chair, place your feet flat on the ground. If you feel comfortable doing so, close your eyes. Take a few deep breaths, feeling the rise of your chest with each inhale and the fall with each exhale. Continue like this until you feel relaxed, grounded, and ready to begin.

Focus your attention on your right toes . . . right foot . . . right calf and shin . . . right knee . . . right thigh . . . right hip . . . abdomen . . . chest . . . right fingers . . . right hand . . . right forearm . . . right elbow . . . right upper arm . . . right shoulder . . . neck . . . throat . . . mouth . . . lips . . . nose . . . eyes . . . forehead . . . crown of the head . . . back of the head . . . nape of the neck . . . upper back . . . left shoulder . . . left upper arm . . . left elbow . . . left forearm . . . left hand . . . left fingers . . . lower back . . . left hip . . . buttocks . . . left thigh . . . left knee . . . left calf and shin . . . left foot . . . left toes . . .

Close the meditation with a few deep breaths. Feel your lungs fill with each inhale, and with each exhale, imagine that the air you took in is spreading to all the corners of your body.

If there is an area of your body that is demanding your attention, imagine yourself sending your breath there, and notice whether the sensation changes. Take as much time as you need to slowly come out of the meditation.

REFLECTION

Were there any particularly interesting sensations you noticed while completing the body scan? Describe the sensations and where you felt them in your body.

....

....

....

....

If you felt any discomfort, did you have the urge to lessen or change the sensation, or make it go away? What was it like to focus on noticing and observing the sensation as opposed to changing it?

....

....

....

....

Optional: A body scan can be a regular part of your mindfulness practice. Each time you complete a scan, you may want to take notes in a journal to compare and contrast your experiences.

Food, Our Fuel

Do you eat to live or live to eat? I personally fall into the latter category. I love trying new foods, flavors, and dishes, and when I travel, my plans often center on where to eat.

For those who eat to live, however, eating may feel like another item on the to-do list, like brushing your teeth or getting dressed. Some may wish that they could give up eating altogether—we make over 200 decisions about food per day on average, so not eating would clear up a lot of brain space. This is what makes dieting and fasting so appealing for some people; instead of having to think about what, when, or how much to eat, the decision has already been made for them.

Although we often just think of food in terms of its effects on our weight, food gives us the energy to move, think, breathe, and *live*. Given that food is so vital to our physical and mental health, our body has multiple ways to indicate this important need. We'll explore these cues in the following sections.

> "First we eat, then we do everything else."
> —*M.F.K. Fisher*

Types of Hunger

In chapter 1, you learned that there are many reasons why we eat, so naturally it follows that there would be different types of hunger driving those reasons. While we are often taught that we should only eat when we're physically hungry, there is really no type of hunger that is "better" than the other, and all are valid reasons to need and eat food.

PHYSICAL, OR "STOMACH" HUNGER

When we think of the word "hunger," we are usually referring to physical hunger. Hunger is regulated by several gut hormones; for example, when the stomach is empty, the hormones motilin and ghrelin act on the brain and gut, stimulating contractions in the stomach and giving us the hungry feeling.

I often have clients who tell me they "never feel hungry" or they "never feel full." Though the sensations of physical hunger are often located around the stomach and abdomen, other signs such as shakiness, dizziness, headaches, increased thoughts about food, or mood changes can all indicate physical hunger.

It's also possible for people to lose touch with their hunger and fullness cues as a result of health conditions or medications, or if they've been repeatedly overriding/ignoring their cues for a long time. In those who frequently skip meals, it's thought that not feeling hungry may be a survival mechanism: the body thinks that it's in famine, so it suppresses the feelings of hunger, giving you the "energy" to hunt for food instead of moaning about how hungry you are. I've had many clients find that they actually feel hungrier the more they eat, as previously suppressed signals come back "online."

DESIRE, OR "BRAIN" HUNGER

When we talk about "cravings," what we are really describing is brain hunger, or wanting to eat for reasons that are more psychological (thinking) than physical (feeling/sensing). Brain hunger can sometimes be distinguished from stomach hunger based on a desire for a specific food or a lack of physical sensations, though that is not always the case.

Because brain hunger is based on thoughts, we sometimes have more control over it than other types of hunger. Here are some examples:

- Eating at a scheduled mealtime or break time, despite not feeling physically hungry
- Eating at a party or celebration
- Eating something because of its health benefits
- Eating to try something new
- Eating something you might not get elsewhere

EMOTIONAL, OR "HEART" HUNGER

Sometimes regarded as a subset of brain hunger, heart hunger is when we are looking to food to fill an emotional need. As discussed in chapter 1, food is meant to bring us pleasure in order to motivate us to seek it out, so that we won't starve. Knowing that food gives us a natural pick-me-up, it makes sense that we would eat to escape or soothe the discomfort of being sad, angry, anxious, etc., or to reinforce the joy of a celebration.

TASTE, OR "MOUTH" HUNGER

Have you ever thought to yourself, "I feel like something sweet," or "I'm craving something crunchy"? The desire for a specific taste or texture is sometimes described as mouth hunger. Like heart hunger, mouth hunger is sometimes considered a subtype of brain hunger. Mouth hunger and heart hunger are often closely linked, as we tend to associate certain flavors and foods with different memories and emotions. (See "The Metaphor of Cravings" on page 56.)

EXERCISE: WHY AM I HUNGRY?

Because different types of hunger often overlap, it's sometimes difficult to tease them apart. You may feel brain *and* stomach hunger if you wake up craving bacon and eggs for breakfast. You may feel stomach *and* heart hunger after a stressful day at work with no breaks. The purpose of this exercise is not to point out that there is a right or wrong time to eat; rather, it's to highlight how complex hunger and appetite can be.

You may choose to complete this activity over the course of a day, or at times when you are eating outside of your regular meals and snacks. The first row has been completed as an example.

Time	Place/Situation	Type of Hunger				Body Sensations	Notes
		STOMACH	BRAIN	HEART	MOUTH		
5:30 p.m.	Out on a first date		x	x		Nervous— "butterflies in stomach"	Earlier than usual dinnertime, so not physically hungry. Ordered a meal mainly to calm my nerves, and so it wouldn't seem like I was watching my date eat

REFLECTION

What type(s) of hunger tend to show up most often for you?

....

What are some of the similarities and differences between how the different types of hunger feel in your body?

....

....

....

....

How do the different types of hunger affect what or how much you eat, if at all?

....

....

....

....

Your Fullness Signals

Now that we've explored hunger, let's talk about the opposite end of the spectrum: fullness. As a result of diet culture, we've come to develop a complicated relationship with fullness and satiety. Instead of seeing fullness as a sign of having had enough to eat, many diets teach that feeling full is a sign we've eaten too much. So we turn to diet plans and food lists to tell us how much we should eat instead of trusting our own cues.

On the other hand, there are many ways we've been taught to override and eat past our fullness cues. Most of us can relate to being told by our parents that we need to finish everything on our plates before we're allowed to have dessert, or trying to get our money's worth at an all-you-can-eat buffet. With growing environmental concerns around food waste, there is also more societal pressure to be part of the "clean plate club." When you become familiar with your fullness signals, you'll have more information to help you decide when to stop eating.

SATIETY

Like hunger, fullness is regulated by a variety of hormones, including leptin from our fat cells and glucagon-like peptide 1 (GLP-1) and cholecystokinin (CCK) from our small bowel. These hormones signal to our body when there is an influx of energy and nutrients from food, instructing our body to digest and absorb what is there, while decreasing appetite and the urge to eat more. Nerves and neurons in our digestive system also play a role, detecting the physical stretching of our stomach and intestines as food travels through our digestive tract.

FEELING AND ACKNOWLEDGING FULLNESS

Because many of us have a history of avoiding and/or ignoring our fullness cues, learning to feel and acknowledge them again can be difficult and uncomfortable. Mindful eating can help you sit with this discomfort and rebuild your relationship with this natural and normal body sensation. Here is how my Four Mindfulness Practice Principles (see page 7) can help you feel and acknowledge your fullness:

Press Pause and Be Present. Before you begin eating, ground yourself by taking a few deep breaths or saying grace if it's part of your religious or spiritual tradition. Throughout the meal, remind yourself to be present and check in with the sensations in your body. An external cue, like putting your fork down every few bites, can be helpful.

Sensing, Not Slowing. Fullness is generally felt as a pressure or heaviness in the stomach and/or abdomen, though, like hunger, it may appear in other parts of the body. Some people notice that they start burping as they're getting full, while others notice that they feel happier and calmer or that the food doesn't taste as good, even without any particular gut sensations.

It can take about 20 minutes for our stomach to signal to our brain that it's full. If you typically take less than 20 minutes to finish eating, consider experimenting with slowing your pace of eating to allow yourself to notice the nuances in the sensation of fullness.

Curiosity, Not Judgment. Sometimes you may feel guilty or ashamed if you eat past fullness or feel annoyed if you get hungry again after you've just eaten. You might be thinking, "I've been eating all my life! Food is a basic need! Why am I not getting this?"

If attuning to your hunger and fullness cues is a new skill for you, remember that you are simultaneously unlearning a lifelong habit of ignoring or overriding these cues. Treat yourself with patience and compassion. Also remember that the idea of only eating when hungry and stopping when full is an idea that comes from diet culture—there is no right or wrong time or amount to eat, and all of this is part of your learning process.

Practice, Not Perfection. Try to practice feeling and acknowledging your fullness regularly, especially in different situations, like eating away from home or eating with others versus alone. The goal is not to find the best situation where you're least likely to eat past fullness. Instead, it's about getting curious and observing how different scenarios can affect your eating habits and hunger/fullness cues.

OVEREATING VERSUS BINGE EATING

Though often uncomfortable, eating past the point of fullness, or overeating, is normal. It's often painted as a "bad" behavior or something to avoid due to its link with weight gain, but as discussed in chapter 1, many different factors contribute to weight and health, and the link between the two is often conflated in our society. Still, many people avoid overeating due to physical discomfort.

Binge eating is different from overeating. In the *Diagnostic and Statistical Manual of Mental Disorders*, 5th Edition (DSM-5), the reference used by medical professionals for diagnosing mental health conditions, "binge eating" is defined as eating a much larger amount of food than what most people would eat under similar circumstances and in a similar time frame (usually defined as two hours) in a way that feels out of control. Because it is associated with feelings of distress, shame, and guilt, binge eating is often done in secret. In chapter 3, you'll learn a bit more about binge eating disorder and bulimia nervosa, two eating disorders that are associated with binge eating.

It's unknown what exactly causes binge eating. Risk factors include irregular eating patterns, significant weight changes, experiences of weight stigma, trauma, and other mental disorders, and specific triggers vary.

If you are struggling with binge eating, I invite you to extend some compassion toward yourself. You are not "wrong" or "broken" for binge eating. Like other "problematic" behaviors, it's often a sign that you're trying to cope with something but perhaps lack the resources to do so in a more sustainable way. Talk to a doctor or other healthcare professional who may be able to refer you to the resources to get the help you need. Alternately, national organizations such as the National Eating Disorders Association often have a 24-hour helpline and can link you to resources in your area. (See the Resources on page 161.)

Some of the tools shared in this workbook can be helpful for managing binge eating. In chapter 3, you can try the "Urge Surfing" exercise (see page 52), which can help reduce the urge to binge. If afterward you still feel the desire to binge, give yourself permission and challenge yourself to do so as mindfully as possible. While these exercises may not stop the binges entirely, they are meant to help you experience the binges in a different way, which may open up space to help you manage them, ideally with professional help.

EXERCISE: THE HUNGER-FULLNESS SCALE

I often use the Hunger-Fullness Scale with my clients as a tool to ground the practice of attuning to your internal cues. Often when we talk about hunger and fullness, it is presented as a dichotomy: You're hungry or you're full. In reality, there is a spectrum of physical sensations that you may experience.

A Hunger-Fullness Scale appears below. Some people like to use numbers to gauge their level of hunger or fullness, while others resonate more with the descriptive words.

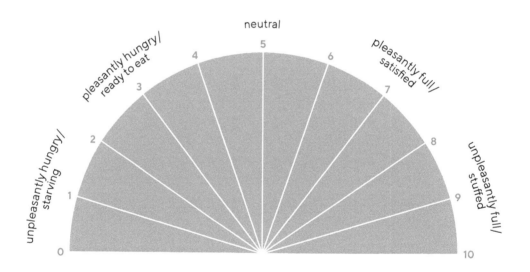

USING THE HUNGER-FULLNESS SCALE

Each person's hunger and fullness cues will be different. Use the Hunger-Fullness Scale as a guide. The next time you are about to eat, check in and ask yourself, "Where am I on the Hunger-Fullness Scale right now?"

Once you've decided, ask yourself, "How is my body telling me that I am at X on the Hunger-Fullness Scale?" Jot down some of the sensations you feel on the corresponding space on the scale. Repeat this at the end of your meal.

Continue this process over several days until you have a descriptor for each area of the scale. Doing this is not meant to change your eating habits or prevent you from eating; rather, it's to help you get into the practice of observing your hunger and fullness cues.

You will likely notice that many different factors contribute to your hunger and fullness. While you may reach a certain point of fullness from a meal on one day, you may have a completely different experience on another. Allow yourself to experiment and simply be curious without judgment.

REFLECTION

Once you become more familiar with your hunger and fullness cues, here are some questions to consider:

What are the similarities and differences between the different levels of hunger and fullness? Do some sensations only appear in certain cases?

....

....

What happens if you start eating at a lower point on the scale (i.e., hungrier) than you normally do? What if you start at a higher point (i.e., fuller)?

....

....

What happens if you stop eating at a lower point on the scale (i.e., hungrier) than you normally do? What if you stop at a higher point (i.e., fuller)?

....

....

How do different levels of hunger affect what and how much you eat, if at all?

....

....

Stop Fighting Your Body: Ditch the Diets

Though the word "diet" technically means any pattern of eating, in our culture dieting has come to be synonymous with attempts to lose weight. I know it might seem a bit contradictory to have a *dietitian* tell you to "ditch the diets," but there are actually a growing number of us adopting a non-diet/anti-diet approach. The following discussions explain why.

MORE THAN FAD DIETS

When I first heard of the terms "non-diet" and "anti-diet," I thought it meant "non-fad-diet" or "anti-fad-diet," which I think most dietitians can get behind. While I fully respect an individual's autonomy in choosing what works best for them, I personally wouldn't push a keto diet, intermittent fasting, or any other "quick fix" on my clients.

However, I've come to realize that "diet" in this case really means any intentional weight loss. There is strong evidence that most people who try to lose weight, even by making what are considered sensible lifestyle changes, will ultimately regain weight, with up to two-thirds of them gaining more weight than they had lost.

THE EFFECTS OF ADVERTISING AND OTHER EXTERNAL CUES TO EAT

Advertising very obviously affects the way we spend and live—why else would companies spend so much money and resources on it? Interestingly, however, a 2016 review published in the *American Journal of Clinical Nutrition* found that short-term exposure to food advertising (i.e., ad breaks in a TV show or movie) seems to cause children, but not adults, to eat more. (That's not to say we aren't affected by it, too.)

Can mindful eating help us overcome external influences to eat, such as advertising, large portions, or even pushy relatives? Yes and no. Some people find that using mindfulness to focus on their inner cues can help them recognize their own needs and tune out those external voices. However, just as discussed in "Mindful Eating and Weight" on page 8, when we are focused on a future outcome in our eating, it pulls us from the present moment and can add an element of judgment (i.e., if we "give in" to the advertising).

Mindful eating is about simply acknowledging that our eating is influenced by both internal and external factors, and being able to sit with this knowledge with curiosity, not judgment. Sometimes you will notice that your choice to eat is mostly influenced by internal cues, like hunger and fullness, while other times, you will notice that it is influenced more by external cues. Either way, it's not right or wrong.

According to the set-point theory, this is because our body tries to keep our weight within a set range that is mostly influenced by genetics. When we lose weight, even when it's intentional, our body thinks it's starving to death and does everything it can to conserve energy—metabolism slows, the levels of gut hormones change to encourage a bigger appetite, etc. The well-known "Biggest Loser" study showed that these effects can be long-lasting; past contestants of *The Biggest Loser* show were found to have a slower metabolism six years after they'd been on the show compared to before the competition, even after they'd gained all the weight back. When you try to lose weight, you are essentially fighting your body.

Some argue that although statistically intentional weight loss is not effective for most people, we should still try. The problem is, intentional weight loss is not without its harms. It's correlated with weight cycling (yo-yo dieting), distorted body image, and disordered eating. While studies have shown that mindful eating is correlated with lower weights, when it comes down to the individual level, it's impossible to predict whether you will gain weight, lose weight, or stay the same weight as a result of adopting a mindful eating practice.

THE REAL FIGHT AGAINST WEIGHT STIGMA

The desire to lose weight doesn't happen in a vacuum. It comes from the fact that we live in a society that thinks of fat and weight gain as negatives and idealizes thinner bodies over larger bodies. A growing amount of research shows that weight stigma itself can contribute to poor physical and mental health, regardless of weight.

Studies show that people in larger bodies are viewed as lazy, incompetent, lacking self-control, and having poor hygiene by employers, teachers, and the public alike. People in larger bodies are less likely to seek medical help due to negative experiences with weight stigma in healthcare settings, and the focus of visits is often on their weight, not the medical issues at hand.

Weight stigma is more than how larger people are viewed or treated by others; our public spaces are often not accommodating for larger bodies. Chairs often don't fit people of larger size, and narrow doors and hallways can be difficult to navigate, limiting access and contributing to the marginalization of people on the higher end of the weight spectrum.

MANAGING YOUR EATING FOR HEALTH REASONS

A question that often comes up in this discussion is, "What if you have legitimate health concerns?" For example, is it okay to follow a low-sodium diet if you have high blood pressure? Or the Mediterranean diet if you are concerned about heart health?

WHY EATING IS LIKE PACKING A SUITCASE

Packing is one of my least favorite activities, so it's ironic that it's one of my favorite analogies for eating. I know people roll their eyes every time they hear a dietitian say, "All foods fit," or, "Everything in moderation," so this analogy gives it a refreshing spin.

There's no wrong way to pack a suitcase. Most people pack the same essentials: underwear, a toothbrush, prescription medication, a change of clothes or two. Each person has their own "extras" that they like—that shirt that never wrinkles or a good book for the plane. Some people have hacks to fit as much as they can in their suitcase without going over the size or weight limit, or to make sure that everything is all neat and organized. Still, at the end of the day, there's nothing stopping you from just stuffing your suitcase full of shoes and heading off on your way.

Of course, most people would probably rather see the sights than spend their entire trip shopping for new underwear and toothpaste, but it's your choice how you want to pack your suitcase. Likewise, there's no wrong way to eat. Sure, there are dietary essentials we need to survive; even so, our bodies are diverse and resilient, and we are able to survive and thrive even when we're not meeting the guidelines for the different nutrients.

Just like your suitcase doesn't contain the exact same items every time you travel, you don't eat the exact same things every time you eat, and it still works. Sometimes it's frustrating when we eat something that doesn't make us feel good, just like it's frustrating when we forget to pack something. It doesn't make us wrong or bad; we just figure it out and move on.

Of course! You always have the right to choose how you take care of your body. At the same time, I invite you to use the awareness and curiosity you cultivate with mindful eating to question whether some of these food rules are necessary. If you have been given specific dietary recommendations from your healthcare team, such as a gluten-free diet for celiac disease, the answer is probably yes. But, in many other cases, while nutrition research can tell us what "works" for many people in a controlled environment, you may need to do some experimenting to figure out what works best for your physical *and* mental health. Seeking out a dietitian, particularly one who specializes in mindful eating, intuitive eating, and/ or Health At Every Size® may be helpful. (You can find more information on the latter approach on page 94.)

Appreciating Yourself

A common belief is that "we are our own worst critics." At the same time, the concepts of self-love and self-compassion have been gaining traction in recent years. Where do mindfulness and mindful eating fit in with all of this? By focusing on nonjudgment and observing from a neutral perspective, mindfulness can open up space for us to reframe negative, critical thoughts into neutral or positive ones.

AVOID COMPARISON

Theodore Roosevelt once said, "Comparison is the thief of joy." It's so easy for us to slip into what I call "compare and despair mode," lamenting and criticizing ourselves over how we're not "good enough."

As naturally social beings, it makes sense we would want to compare ourselves to others as benchmarks to make sure we fit in. This is similar to how we have a tendency to rely on external cues, like an empty plate or a diet plan, to help us decide what and how much to eat. When we use mindfulness and mindful eating to help us shift toward our internal cues, we can get a better sense of what we truly need and are capable of, no matter what others do or think.

FORGIVE SETBACKS

Perfectionism is similar to comparison, except instead of benchmarking yourself against someone else, you are comparing yourself to a standard or expectation you've created. A setback is really just an expectation that has not been met.

When it comes to mindful eating, some of my clients feel frustrated that they are "still" eating past fullness, eating with distractions, not 100 percent present in the moment, or just struggling to "get it" for any other reason. I generally start with the reminder that mindful eating is a new skill they are learning while undoing a lifetime of not eating mindfully; it is a lifelong practice, not something to be perfected. I also use the situation as an invitation to revisit some of the expectations people might have and reframe them into thoughts that might be more realistic:

- Are these expectations realistic given the context of your current life situation?
- What can you learn from the fact that expectations are not being met?
- How can you reframe these expectations so they are more achievable?

PRACTICE GRATITUDE

Sometimes we move through life so quickly and mindlessly that it can be easy to take things for granted. In a sense, practicing gratitude is like a mindfulness practice, as it cues us to slow down and appreciate all that is around us. Some people find it helpful to keep a gratitude journal and list what they are grateful for every day.

As you learn to become more present and aware of the external things you are grateful for, you will find opportunities to turn inward and appreciate your body and yourself. When was the last time you thanked your body for keeping you alive, instead of lamenting over its appearance and shape? What would it be like to feel gratitude for your body instead of constantly looking for areas for improvement?

EXERCISE: THE LAST TIME YOU ATE

Use the following prompts to help you reflect on the last time you ate and write your responses in the space provided:

- When and where was the last time you ate?
- What made you decide to eat?
- What did you eat? (Describe it using all your senses: sight, smell, hearing, taste, and touch.)
- What thoughts and emotions came up as you were eating?
- What else was happening while you were eating (i.e., conversation, watching TV, reading, working, etc.)?
- How did you decide when to stop eating?
- What thoughts and emotions came up when you were finished eating?

Review your responses to the "Last Time You Ate" exercise on page 14. What are some similarities and differences between your eating experiences? How has learning more about the connections between mindful eating, embodiment, interoceptive awareness, dieting, and self-appreciation changed the way you eat, if at all?

....

....

....

....

Chapter Check-in

In this chapter, you learned about the role of hunger and fullness in mindful eating, how mindful eating fits in a non-diet/anti-diet approach, and the connections between mindfulness, self-compassion, self-love, and gratitude.

What are some of your aha moments from this chapter? What are some areas you'd like to focus on as you continue to learn and build your practice?

....

....

....

....

....

CHAPTER THREE

IN YOUR BRAIN

Our eating habits are influenced by more than just our hunger and fullness cues. Our brain plays a role, too. In fact, our feelings, thoughts, desires, and even the environment around us can influence how we eat. In this chapter, you'll have an opportunity to examine how these factors may influence you, as well as some of the challenges you may encounter and how you might approach them.

Your Brain on Food

We often focus so much on the effect food can have on our body that we forget that food also feeds our brain. Our brain makes up about 20 percent of our total energy needs—more than any other organ in our body. Most of the time, our brain relies solely on glucose (sugar) for energy, as it is the only form of energy from food that can pass the blood-brain barrier. When the body is starved of glucose, it goes into ketosis, which is when the liver is forced to break down fatty acids to form ketones for energy. Ketones are also able to cross the blood-brain barrier to feed the brain.

When the brain is seeking energy, it can manifest as changes in our thoughts and feelings around food. For example, some people find that thinking about food is one of their first signs of hunger, even before other body cues. Others notice that their mood changes when they get hungry . . . or "hangry," so to speak. Many people who adopt a low-carb diet experience what is called "keto flu," a cluster of symptoms that include irritability, dizziness, difficulty concentrating, and brain fog, as the brain is starved of nutrients before the body produces enough ketones to feed it again.

DESIRE AND CRAVINGS

As you've learned, food is more than fuel; it's absolutely normal and healthy to desire and derive pleasure from food. Unfortunately, diet culture has taught us to not trust those desires—we're taught to follow meal plans, calorie counts, and other food rules, overriding our body's cues. Furthermore, words like "desire" and "pleasure" are often sexualized, adding to the "forbidden" nature of cravings.

As a result, when it comes to cravings, our instinct is to clamp down, tighten the reins, and tell ourselves we can't give in. The more we tell ourselves we can't do something, the more we want to do it. So we end up trying to "eat around our cravings," only to be left unsatisfied and have the craving continue to grow. Finally, we end up eating what we were craving to begin with, as illustrated in the figure on the next page.

When this happens, we often end up eating uncontrollably, partly because the craving is likely more intense than when it started; partly because at this point we're upset with ourselves for being "weak" and breaking our food rules; and partly because we promise ourselves that this is the last time, and after this, we will never give in again. We clamp down and tighten the reins harder, leaving ourselves trapped in the diet-binge cycle.

ACCEPTING YOUR CRAVINGS

As you might have guessed by now, it's impossible to stop cravings permanently. Cravings are simply one way our body communicates a need. In fact, the secret

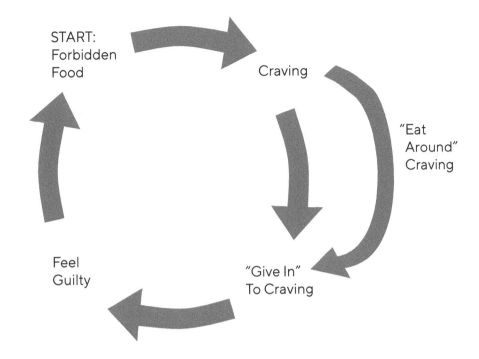

START:
Forbidden
Food

Craving

"Eat
Around"
Craving

Feel
Guilty

"Give In"
To Craving

to breaking free from the diet-binge cycle is to **give yourself permission to satisfy your cravings**.

You might be thinking, "No way! If I gave in to my cravings, I would just eat junk food all the time!" You're right—it's normal that when you initially give yourself permission, you will probably overeat because your body is "making up for lost time." Your body might also subconsciously anticipate that you'll go back to restricting again, so you eat with a "last supper" mentality.

So why should you give yourself permission to satisfy your cravings if you're probably going to overeat?

Reframing the language from "giving in" to "satisfying" your cravings shifts the power from the craving back to you. Instead of trying to use willpower to resist your cravings, mindfulness can give you the space to get curious about the craving and the power to choose how you want to satisfy it. Perhaps you don't feel physically hungry, but the craving is likely signaling another physical, emotional, or social need. You may then choose to satisfy the craving directly by eating the food or satisfy the need in another way.

Giving yourself permission to satisfy your cravings might help decrease their frequency and intensity through the process of habituation. As your body becomes used to the idea that you *do* have permission to eat, and that the food won't be taken away, the food and craving start to lose their power and emotional charge.

It's like saying "I love you" to a partner: The first time you say, "I love you," there is probably a lot of emotional buildup in terms of picking just the right time and place to say it. Over time, it's almost as easy to say, "I love you," as it is to say, "Hello." That doesn't mean the phrase has lost its meaning; it just doesn't have that same emotional impact anymore. Similarly, habituation is not about eating so much of the food that you get sick of it; it's about taking it off the pedestal and treating it as "just food."

EXERCISE: URGE SURFING

Urge surfing is a mindfulness technique developed by psychologist G. Alan Marlatt. Though Dr. Marlatt's specialty was in addictions, this strategy can be used for any type of urge, including food cravings.

Imagine you are swimming in the ocean and a wave starts to form. It starts out small, but it quickly grows in size, and you soon feel overwhelmed. You muster up all your strength to swim against the wave, pushing your body forward with your arms and legs, fighting to keep yourself from being pulled under. Eventually, almost as suddenly as the wave appeared, it begins to subside. Soon, you find yourself swimming in calm waters again.

Like a wave, a craving often starts as a whisper, and then quickly becomes more intense, until it feels as though all your thoughts are occupied by the food. Often this is the point where you'd likely give in or try to find another way to get rid of the discomfort. Urge surfing is like using your breath as a "surfboard" to face the discomfort head-on and ride the wave of the craving. It helps you recognize that your cravings are only temporary, and that they will eventually subside.

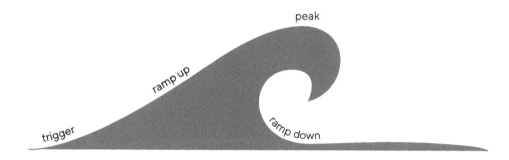

The following meditation can help you "surf the urge," so that you can practice responding differently when you experience a craving. You may want to record yourself reading the following passage, allowing enough time to follow the instructions as you read, and then play it back so that you can stay present in the activity.

Settle comfortably in your seat. If you are sitting in a chair, place your feet flat on the ground. If you feel comfortable doing so, close your eyes. Take a few deep breaths, feeling the rise of your chest with each inhale and the fall with each exhale. Continue like this until you feel ready to begin.

Turn your attention to your craving. Notice where it is located in your body: You may notice it in your head . . . mouth . . . throat . . . neck . . . chest . . . hands. There is no right or wrong place to feel a craving. If you feel your craving in multiple areas of your body, turn to the place where it feels most intense first.

Notice the physical sensation of your craving without judgment. Get curious: What does it feel like? Does it feel like tightness, pressure, tingling, or something else? Is it warm, cool, or in between? Does the area have a well-defined shape, or is it like a fuzzy aura? If it is becoming overwhelming to notice your sensations, turn your attention back to your breath, focusing on the sensation of each inhale and exhale, until you feel grounded and comfortable. Then turn your attention back to your craving when you are able.

As you continue to breathe, notice how your craving changes from moment to moment, if at all. Just as you can't make a wave any smaller, there is no need to try to change your craving. Simply observe with each cycle of breath without judgment. If you notice your mind wandering, gently guide yourself back to feeling your craving. (Or to your breath, if your craving is too overwhelming.)

Take as much time as you need to continue feeling and observing your craving and breathing. If there are other parts of your body that are feeling the craving, move on to those when you are ready.

When you are ready to finish this meditation, open your eyes and take a moment to notice how you feel before moving on to the rest of your day.

REFLECTION

Describe and/or draw the physical sensation of your craving. Where was it located? What did it feel and/or look like?

How did your craving change as you continued to breathe, if at all?

....

....

....

....

How did you feel at the end of the meditation?

....

....

....

....

If at the end of this urge surfing activity, you still feel the urge to eat, **go ahead and eat**. Remember that **you didn't do anything wrong**. Sometimes a craving may last much longer or be more intense than you anticipated. Sometimes urge surfing just doesn't fit with your current situation. **The point is not to stop yourself from eating**. Instead, it's to use your cravings as an opportunity to get curious and practice responding to them in a different, more purposeful way.

THE METAPHOR OF CRAVINGS

More often than not, cravings reflect an emotional need. In her book, *Eating in the Light of the Moon*, psychologist Anita A. Johnston proposes that we subconsciously use food as a metaphor. For example, many comfort foods, like tomato soup or hot chocolate, are warm, perhaps symbolizing a need for emotional warmth. Craving sweets, like candy or ice cream, may be a sign that we are searching for sweetness in our life or in ourselves, while crunchy foods are a metaphor for being angry or frustrated. Depending on your memories and experiences, you may have your own personal meanings for different foods.

Emotions and Eating

Virtually every human on the planet has engaged in emotional eating at one time or another. Emotional eating is typically associated with unpleasant emotions like sadness, anger, stress, and boredom, but pleasant emotions like celebration, curiosity, and excitement can also trigger eating.

As with cravings, emotional eating often gets a bad rap because of the idea that we "shouldn't" be eating more than we "need." In reality, food is a relatively harmless method of emotion regulation (compared to, say, alcohol or drugs) that is readily available for most people. Of course, the effects of food are temporary and often don't address what caused the emotion in the first place, so it can be helpful to practice other coping mechanisms.

FEELING YOUR FEELINGS

Emotions are also called "feelings" for a reason; each emotion comes with a physical sensation. You've probably heard of "having butterflies in your stomach," or "having a gut feeling" about something. It's no coincidence that we connect so many of our emotions with our gut. Research on the gut-brain axis—or the communication between the nerves in the digestive system and the central nervous system in the brain—shows that our digestive system does a lot more than tell our brain when we're hungry or full; even early research in the nineteenth century found that our mood can affect our gut function.

More recent research shows that stress can affect secretions, movement, and blood flow in our gut, just to name a few. Knowing this, it makes a little more sense why emotional eating is so common; not only are we responding to an emotional trigger, but the physical sensations we feel can sometimes mimic hunger.

EXERCISE: YOUR EMOTIONS IN COLOR

Get some different colored pens, markers, or pencils: things are about to get colorful! This activity will help you get a better sense of the physical sensations associated with your emotions.

1. Choose an emotion from the following list and circle it with a specific color, or write your own emotion in one of the spaces provided.
2. Using the same color, mark or circle the area of your body where you feel this emotion on the silhouette.
3. Using the same color, on the lines below the silhouette, describe specifics about the sensation (i.e., tingling, pressure, pain) and whether you feel the sensation is pleasant, unpleasant, or neutral.
4. Repeat with as many emotions and colors as you wish.

Happy	Sad	Angry	Bored	Stressed
Tired	Uncomfortable	Upset	Scared	Worried

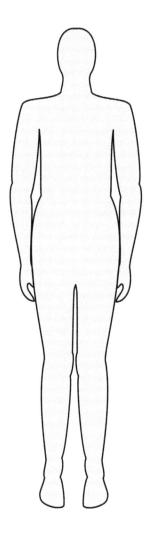

. . . .

. . . .

. . . .

. . . .

. . . .

ACKNOWLEDGING EMOTIONAL TRIGGERS

As we've discussed so far in this chapter, there are many ways our emotions can affect our eating habits. Our emotions can trigger cravings in the presence or absence of physical hunger; they can also trigger physical sensations that can be confused with hunger. Later in this chapter, we'll use the cognitive behavioral therapy (CBT) model to show how our emotions can both directly influence our eating behaviors, and indirectly influence our thoughts of eating.

Why is it so important for us to understand all these different ways that our emotions can affect our eating? Conventional wisdom would argue that we need to understand a problem before we can solve it; however, throughout this workbook we've talked about how emotional eating is actually a normal part of our life, not something that we need to fix or stop.

Since mindfulness is about being fully aware in the present moment, having this knowledge simply gives us more to think about and explore when it comes to the eating experience. When we are able to experience our emotional eating without judgment, we can have a better understanding of our emotional needs and perhaps come up with alternative ways to meet them if we choose.

SEPARATING YOUR EMOTIONS FROM YOUR EATING

Because emotional eating is often seen as "negative" or "wrong," we are sometimes told that we should separate our emotions from our eating—that we should only "eat to live," and never "live to eat." Not only is this impossible, but the fact that food can affect our emotions can actually make our meals more satisfying. For example, eating a meal prepared by a loved one will probably feel more comforting than ordering takeout. Having a chocolate bar will probably feel more rewarding and soothing than a stick of celery after a stressful day.

That being said, not all meals are going to be amazing, positive experiences—sometimes you are just "eating to live." The practice of mindful eating is about being present in all eating experiences without judgment, whether they are unpleasant, pleasant, or neutral, as well as having the space to act in response however you choose.

Time	Location	How You Feel Before Eating	What You Ate	How You Feel During/After Eating	Pleasant/ Unpleasant/ Neutral	Additional Notes
12 p.m.	Desk at work	Hungry, stressed	Turkey sandwich, baby carrots, chocolate bar	No longer hungry but could eat more, still stressed	Unpleasant	Didn't really pay attention to my food because I was worried about work. Didn't plan to eat chocolate bar, but I didn't feel full yet. Not sure if this is stomach or heart hunger.

EXERCISE: HOW DO YOU FEEL WHEN YOU EAT?

This exercise will help you identify some of the factors that may be influencing your eating habits. You may fill out the worksheet on the previous page over the course of a day, or you may choose to only do this activity when you notice that you are eating emotionally.

REFLECTION

After reviewing your completed worksheet, what, if any, patterns or potential triggers do you notice?

....

....

....

....

....

Eating Disorders and Disordered Eating

Though mainstream media sometimes portrays eating disorders as "extreme dieting" or "emotional eating gone wrong," eating disorders are a mental condition, not a choice. They can affect people of all ages, races, and sizes. The current diagnostic criteria for eating disorders come from the *Diagnostic and Statistical Manual of Mental Disorders*, 5th Edition (DSM-5). The three most well-known eating disorders are anorexia nervosa, bulimia nervosa, and binge eating disorder.

ANOREXIA NERVOSA

The diagnostic criteria for anorexia nervosa are distorted body image, fear of weight gain, and restriction of energy intake leading to low body weight. It affects about 0.9 percent of women and 0.3 percent of men. Anorexia nervosa is the most fatal of all eating disorders (which are already the most fatal mental condition), partly due to some of the medical consequences of suppressed weight.

BULIMIA NERVOSA

Bulimia nervosa is characterized by repeated episodes of binge eating (on average, at least once weekly over three months) and compensatory behaviors—such as vomiting, laxative use, or excessive exercise—in response to the binges, with the hope of preventing weight gain. Like anorexia nervosa, people with bulimia nervosa have a distorted body image. The condition affects about 1.5 percent of women and 0.5 percent of men.

BINGE EATING DISORDER

Binge eating disorder is a newly recognized eating disorder, having only been defined in 2013, when the DSM-5 was published. It is the most common eating disorder, affecting about 3.5 percent of women and 2 percent of men. Like bulimia nervosa, binge eating disorder involves repeated episodes of binge eating, but without the compensatory behaviors seen in the former.

DISORDERED EATING

Eating disorders are serious business, but disordered eating—when someone engages in problematic eating behaviors in a way that don't meet eating disorder criteria—is more widespread and insidious. A 2008 survey by *SELF* magazine, in partnership with the University of North Carolina at Chapel Hill, found that 75 percent of American women aged 25 to 45 years old reported disordered eating behaviors.

Disordered eating can often be hard to spot as diet culture normalizes and sometimes praises many disordered behaviors. Signs and symptoms include:

- Constantly thinking about food (when it's not part of your job)
- Counting calories, macros, points, etc.
- Restricting foods and food groups (when there is no medical reason)
- Concerns about food impacting your social life
- Binge eating (less than the frequency that would meet eating disorder diagnostic criteria)

GETTING HELP

If you are concerned that you or a loved one is struggling with an eating disorder, many countries have national agencies that can connect you with proper support. In the United States, the National Eating Disorders Association (NEDA) can be reached at 1-800-931-2237 or via their website, nationaleatingdisorders.org.

Your History, Through Food

One of my favorite podcasts is called *Food Psych*. The host, Christy Harrison, begins each interview with, "Tell me about your relationship with food growing up." I have always enjoyed listening to each guest's response because it can reveal a lot about their relationship with food and their body today.

Our relationship with food and with our body can add context to the reasons we eat and the eating experience. Just as our nutritional needs change throughout our various stages of life, so, too, does our relationship with food. As newborns, our relationship with food is pretty straightforward—we eat only one type of food, breast milk or formula; we instinctively know to cry when we're hungry and stop when we're full. From then on, we're bombarded with direct and indirect messages about what, how much, when, and where we should eat. As toddlers, our relationship with food is mostly influenced by our parents and caregivers; as our social circle expands throughout childhood, we receive additional messages from teachers, friends, health professionals, mass media, and so on.

Teenagers are particularly vulnerable to disordered eating and a negative relationship with food, as they navigate increasing independence and responsibilities, as well as the changes in their bodies as they approach adulthood. Though it's normal to gain up to 25 to 40 pounds during puberty, our society often frames all weight gain as "bad," and teens often turn to dieting and restrictive eating as a result.

While our physiological needs are relatively stable throughout adulthood, our relationship with food can still continue to change. Major life events like going to college, moving out, getting our first job, being in different relationships, getting married, having children, retirement, and menopause can influence our relationship with food.

Although mindful eating asks us to be aware of the present moment, I invite you to also consider your "food history" when it comes to better understanding your relationship with food and your body.

A Culture of Distraction

Although slowing down is not a prerequisite to mindfulness and mindful eating, it can be difficult to fully take in and appreciate the eating experience in our fast-paced society without doing so. It's not uncommon for us to eat lunch at our desk (while scrolling through social media on our phone) or to not realize that we've eaten a full bag of chips until our fingers reach the bottom of the bag. These are examples of distracted eating and mindless eating.

DISTRACTED EATING

There's a common belief that we need to eat without any distractions to eat mindfully. But I have a confession to make: I have been eating distractedly for as long as I can remember. Growing up, I was always reading something at breakfast, whether it was a book, a newspaper, or a cereal box. Our TV was always angled toward the kitchen table, so dinner was usually accompanied by the news or the latest drama.

Nowadays, I often eat with my phone in hand, whether it's reading the latest news or playing a game. Does that mean I'm not being mindful? Not necessarily. In my own mindfulness and mindful eating practice, I've tried to frame this as a part of my eating experience, not as a separate distraction. Sometimes, the phone does not take away from the enjoyment of my meal; other times, I notice that I'm so engrossed in it that I can barely taste what I'm eating, so I remind myself to stop and put my phone away for later.

Life isn't without distractions, and while it may be helpful to minimize any distractions as you are beginning to build your practice so that you can focus on your meal, to say that you should eat without distractions would be very limiting. In some cases, for example, if you have trauma around being completely embodied and present, a distraction may actually be helpful. Mindfulness is an invitation to approach distractions with curiosity: What is it like to eat your meal without distractions and vice versa? What, if anything, needs to change to make your meal more pleasant and enjoyable?

MINDLESS EATING

In the 2006 book *Mindless Eating* by marketing professor Brian Wansink, the author details some of the kooky experiments he conducted on how the environment can influence eating behavior. There was the "bad popcorn" study, which showed that moviegoers would eat more popcorn from larger bags than from smaller ones, even when the popcorn was stale, and the "bottomless soup bowl" study, where a bowl was rigged to refill itself to prove that people rely more on external cues (i.e., an empty bowl) versus their fullness cues to determine when to stop eating.

Aside from the fact that Wansink's research methods have been questioned in recent years (as of this writing, 13 of his studies have been retracted, including a study that was retracted twice), his book does not position "mindful eating" as the opposite of "mindless eating." Instead, the "solutions" he offered—using

PRESSING PAUSE ON MINDLESS EATING

Our brain wants to be as efficient as possible, so it's always trying to turn things into habits and run on autopilot. You probably put your seatbelt on right away when you get into a car or hang your jacket in the same place at home and at work. In many ways, this is a good thing—if we always had to be intentional about everything we did, we would be far less productive.

Given that eating is something we've been doing since birth, it's normal for eating to become mindless—we may barely remember what we're eating, let alone how it tastes, and we eat until the food's gone, regardless of how full we feel.

The first of my Four Mindfulness Practice Principles is **Press Pause and Be Present**. Just as stepping on the brakes takes your car out of cruise control, you can disrupt your brain's autopilot by "pressing pause." This pause might come in the form of taking a deep breath; whispering "Pause" or "Stop" to yourself; or some other cue you choose. Think about what cues might be helpful to you in your mindful eating practice.

Though pressing pause is introduced here as a way to put the brakes on mindless eating, it can also be used during or after eating or at any moment of the day as part of your mindfulness practice. Use the pause as a gentle reminder to be aware in the present moment and make any adjustments you need.

smaller plates, buying food in smaller packages—were really about harnessing our mindlessness to trick ourselves into eating less.

When eating mindfully, get curious and try to notice all the different factors that might influence your eating. They might be obvious, like how hungry you feel or how much food is on your plate (or in your soup bowl), or they might be subtle, like the lighting of the room and the emotions of others around you. With mindfulness, you have the power of choice. Rather than trying to mindlessly trick yourself into eating a certain way or ignoring what's going on around you, how will you mindfully respond to these different triggers?

EXERCISE: DISRUPTING THE EATING EXPERIENCE

Changing *how* you eat can take your brain out of eating on autopilot, which can help you be more aware and present in the experience. To get started, choose a disruption from the following list:

- Eating without any distractions
- Eating with your nondominant hand
- Eating something you usually eat with your hands (i.e., a sandwich or wrap) with a knife and fork
- Eating with a different eating utensil, such as eating soup with a fork
- Putting your eating utensil down between bites
- Chewing each bite at least 20 times before swallowing
- Eating dessert before your main course
- Plating your meal beforehand (if you normally serve your meals family-style)
- Serving your meals family-style (if you normally plate your meals before sitting at the table)
- Not finishing all the food on your plate

Begin your meal by grounding yourself with a few deep breaths. Approach your meal with curiosity, and as you eat your meal while engaging in the disruption you chose, notice, without judgment, the information you are receiving from your senses, thoughts, and emotions about your meal. You do not have to continue with your disruption for the entire meal.

REFLECTION

How did the disruption affect your eating experience, if at all?

....

....

....

Did the disruption help you eat more mindfully? Why or why not?

....

....

....

....

Brain Games

CBT is a psychotherapy approach often used in the treatment of eating disorders and other mental health concerns. One of the core principles of CBT is that our thoughts, feelings, and behaviors are linked and can thus influence one another, as illustrated by this graphic:

As anyone who has eaten emotionally can attest, our feelings can definitely trigger our behaviors. We eat when we're sad, mad, stressed, and so on. In turn, our behavior can change our feelings, albeit temporarily, and not always in the way we hope. As a result, we often think that to change our eating, we need to change how we feel. However, we can't just will ourselves to feel a certain way; we need to change something more malleable: our thoughts.

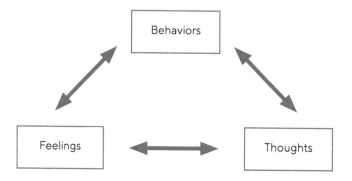

YOU ARE NOT YOUR THOUGHTS

In chapter 1, we briefly touched on how many of us "live in our heads" and allow ourselves to be defined by our thoughts. Mindfulness is one way we can distance ourselves from our thoughts: Instead of following our thoughts as they arise, we focus our attention on the present.

When we define ourselves by our thoughts, it's like we are passengers in a car. We can only see what is directly ahead of us, and we're forced to just go along for the ride. Conversely, mindfulness is like being a bird flying overhead. We can see the car and the possible paths this car can take. We can't change where this car is going or even whether or not it exists. We just acknowledge that it is there, and we can choose to follow it or focus on something else.

CBT also holds that we are not defined by our thoughts, but instead of simply letting them be, CBT invites us to examine them more closely, and if they are negative or unhelpful, we can reframe or respond to them.

IDENTIFYING NEGATIVE THOUGHTS

All of us have negative, unhelpful thoughts from time to time. Sometimes these thoughts are specific to food and eating, like, "Oh, I shouldn't have eaten that," or, "I was bad today because I ate too much." It can also be a more general thought, like, "I'm so lazy," or, "I can't get anything right." These thoughts often feel automatic and can affect our emotions and our behaviors.

Psychologist and meditation teacher Tara Brach uses the acronym RAIN to help us move through challenging thoughts and feelings when they arise:

Recognize what is happening: This is a call to focus on the present. Use your senses to help you capture your surroundings and your body sensations in the moment. Notice the thoughts and feelings that are coming up for you.

Allow the experience to be there, just as it is: This is where the nonjudgment part of mindfulness comes in. When we label a thought as "negative" or "unhelpful," what we are really doing is passing a judgment that reinforces the idea that this thought is something we want to get rid of. When we choose to do the difficult work of sitting with these uncomfortable feelings instead of trying to get rid of them or minimize them in some way, eventually our perspective starts to shift.

> "If you change the way you look at things,
> the things you look at change."
> —*Wayne Dyer*

Investigate with interest, care, and kindness: This is the curiosity part of mindfulness. While it may be tempting to interpret this as finding your triggers and trying to "fix" how you feel, this is about investigating the *present*. You started with recognizing what was happening, but how does this shift from moment to moment? Try to figure out what your body needs through your physical cues, instead of relying on thoughts, which generally live in the past or the future.

Nurture with love and self-compassion: Everyone deserves love and self-compassion, especially after a difficult time. Show yourself a bit of care—it can be as little as placing your hand on your heart and feeling a warmth flow through your body or whispering something kind to yourself.

EXERCISE: CBT-BASED THOUGHT RECORD

In CBT, a thought record can help us become more aware of our negative thoughts so that we can find ways to shift them into more neutral or positive thoughts. You will notice that some of the steps overlap with mindfulness work. As you take these steps, record your responses on the "Thought Record" worksheet on page 73. An example is given on page 72.

Column 1: Acknowledge the situation/identify the trigger: When you notice a negative or unhelpful thought, make note of the situation. Ask yourself the five "Ws"—who, what, where, why, and when—to help you figure out what might have triggered these negative thoughts. (This step incorporates the "R" and "I" of RAIN.)

Column 2: Notice your physical and emotional feelings: What bodily sensations are coming up for you? What emotions are coming up for you? If it is helpful, you can rate the intensity of how you feel on a scale of 1 to 10. (This step also incorporates the "R" of RAIN.)

Column 3: Bring to mind the unhelpful thoughts and images: Often the mean-spirited voice in our head is not very creative and repeats the same phrases over and over again. Allow yourself to replay the tape one more time, so you can get those thoughts down on paper.

Columns 4 and 5: Just the facts: What are the facts that *support* your thought versus the facts that *don't support* them?

Colum 6: Respond to, or reframe, the thought: Given the facts, is your initial thought absolutely true? (Not likely.) How can you respond to your thought in a more reasonable and realistic way? How can you rephrase your thought so that it is more helpful?

Column 7: Reflection: Take note of your physical and emotional feelings again. How have things shifted, if at all?

THOUGHT RECORD

Situation/ Trigger	How do I feel physically and emotionally?	Unhelpful Thoughts/ Images	Facts that support my thoughts	Facts that don't support my thoughts	Respond or Reframe	Reflection (How do I feel physically and emotionally now?)
Giving an important presentation tomorrow.	Stressed and worried. "Butterflies" in stomach, chest.	I won't remember what I have to say. I won't be taken seriously, and I will embarrass myself.	I haven't given this presentation before.	Past presentations I've given have been well received, even when they haven't been "perfect." I've rehearsed this talk several times over the past week.	I feel worried about this presentation because it's important to me. I've done presentations before and they've been well received. I will try my best for this one.	Still a bit nervous but more relieved and confident.

Situation/ Trigger	How do I feel physically and emotionally?	Unhelpful Thoughts/ Images	Facts that support my thoughts	Facts that don't support my thoughts	Respond or Reframe	Reflection (How do I feel physically and emotionally now?)

HOW UNHELPFUL THINKING CAN AFFECT OUR EATING HABITS

In the CBT framework, our thoughts can influence our eating habits either directly (i.e., through desire/cravings or learned behaviors, like time to eat, eating to be polite, etc.) or indirectly through our emotions. When we separate our thoughts from our identity, we can view them more objectively. By reframing or responding to our thoughts, we can change our eating habits.

My client Marie had dieted almost her entire life. She would lose a little bit of weight, then gradually regain, almost always becoming heavier than when she had started, which would lead her to try yet another diet. She was tired of yo-yo dieting but still wished she could lose the weight. Marie was struggling with pain in her joints, which she blamed on her weight, which she in turn blamed on herself.

As a result, Marie would fluctuate between being "good" and eating according to all the diet rules she'd picked up over the years—small portions, unlimited

MORE WAYS TO THINK ABOUT YOUR THOUGHTS AND BEHAVIORS

In the Thought Record on page 73, you were invited to respond to your negative and unhelpful thoughts by questioning whether they were true or false. Other therapy modalities, like dialectical behavior therapy (DBT) and acceptance and commitment therapy (ACT), have different methods for engaging with thoughts and behaviors.

In DBT, which is a form of CBT for managing more intense emotions and harmful behaviors, the emphasis is on whether a thought is helpful or harmful, rather than true or false. Even if a thought is true, if it is still harmful or unhelpful to the person, then it needs to be reframed in a way that is helpful.

ACT encourages people to live according to their values. When different thoughts or behaviors arise, the person can assess whether or not those thoughts or behaviors align with their values, and act accordingly.

vegetables, protein at every meal—then rebelling, breaking all the rules, eating whatever she wanted, and feeling guilty afterward.

Marie and I decided to examine the thought, "I'm in pain because I'm overweight, and I'm overweight because it's my fault." We talked about how both pain and weight are due to a number of factors, many of which are outside of our control. Marie noted that she'd been on many diets where she didn't lose any weight, despite eating very little. After that appointment, Marie met with her chiropractor, who was able to diagnose possible sources of her pain and begin treatment. Being able to take the blame off the weight and thus off of herself gave Marie more clarity to start healing her relationship with food and her body.

EXERCISE: THE LAST TIME YOU ATE

Use the following prompts to help you reflect on the last time you ate, and write your responses in the space provided:

- When and where was the last time you ate?
- What made you decide to eat?
- What did you eat? (Describe it using all your senses: sight, smell, hearing, taste, and touch.)
- What thoughts and emotions came up as you were eating?
- What else was happening while you were eating? (i.e., conversation, watching TV, reading, working, etc.)
- How did you decide when to stop eating?
- What thoughts and emotions came up when you were finished eating?

....

....

....

....

....

Review the "Last Time You Ate" exercises on pages 14 and 46. What are some similarities and differences between your eating experiences? How has learning more about how your emotions can affect your eating habits changed the way you eat, if at all?

....

....

....

....

....

....

....

....

Chapter Check-in

In this chapter, you learned how eating is more than simply responding to your hunger and fullness cues. Your desires, emotions, thoughts, and even the environment can influence the way you eat. By completing the exercises in this chapter, you now have a better idea of how your eating habits are influenced by those factors and how you can change it up if you choose to.

What are some of your aha moments from this chapter? What are some areas you would like to focus on as you continue to learn and build your practice?

....

....

....

....

....

....

CHAPTER FOUR

AT THE TABLE

Now that you've read about the basics of mindfulness and mindful eating, explored the role of your body and brain and how it affects your eating, and reviewed some related concepts and tried out the exercises, it's time to put it all together. This chapter takes you through a "mindful meal"—from preparing the food to swallowing the last bite. We'll also discuss some of the judgments about food and eating that tend to creep in when we talk about enjoyment and nutrition.

The Joy of Eating

Two things are often overlooked in discussions about food and eating: joy and pleasure. In previous chapters, we've discussed how diet culture has led us to believe that joy and pleasure in eating is a "bad" thing. Like exercise, many diets promote a "no pain, no gain" approach to eating, making people feel more superior, pure, and clean when they are able to follow multiple dietary rules and restrictions.

This is one of the reasons why diets don't work—they're miserable! If pleasure motivates us to keep doing something, it makes sense that when something isn't enjoyable, we stop doing it. To turn our eating behaviors into habits, we need to find the joy, the pleasure, and the reward.

SAVOR THE FLAVOR

In many instances, mindful eating can enhance the eating experience. When we are present and use our senses to take in the food we're eating without judgment, we have the opportunity to really taste and get to know our food, instead of eating on autopilot. Many of my clients say that this has helped them get more satisfaction from their eating and learn something new about their connection with food and with their bodies.

Sometimes the satisfaction doesn't necessarily come from the flavor of the food. Other factors that might give us satisfaction include:

- The process of getting and preparing the food
- Supporting a producer or company we like with our dollars
- Enjoying food prepared by a loved one
- Sharing a meal with family and friends
- Getting good service at a restaurant
- Trying a new food or dish
- Eating a food that evokes certain emotions or memories

There are many opportunities to practice mindful eating and to find the joy and satisfaction in the eating experience.

> Mindful eating does not seek perfection because there is no such thing as perfect eating.

IT'S OKAY TO EAT TO LIVE

Though mindful eating often results in getting more satisfaction from our food, as mentioned in chapter 3, not every meal is going to be an exciting, colorful experience. There will be times when you simply need to "eat to live" and can't be completely mindful. There will be times when the meal just isn't good or exciting no matter how much you try to "savor the flavor." There will be times when you will *choose* not to be mindful. Mindful eating does not seek perfection because there is no such thing as perfect eating. It is a lifelong practice.

EXERCISE: HUNGER, FULLNESS, AND SATISFACTION TRACKER

Feeling full is different from feeling satisfied. As mentioned, there are many different parts of a meal that can make it more or less satisfying. For example, most people would probably choose a refreshing iced drink over a hot cocoa on a summer day.

The following tracker will help you continue to practice using the Hunger-Fullness Scale on page 38, as well as notice some of the different factors that play into making a meal satisfying. The first row has been completed as an example.

Time	Hunger/Fullness Rating Before Eating	Food Eaten	Hunger/Fullness Rating After Eating	Satisfaction Rating	Notes
6 p.m.	3	Grilled fish with peach salsa, rice, salad	8	10	Tried a new recipe— very tasty!

REFLECTION

What are some patterns you've noticed in your hunger, fullness, and/or satisfaction ratings, if any?

....

....

....

....

How did your hunger or fullness contribute to your satisfaction ratings,
if at all?

....

....

....

....

What are some factors that tend to contribute to your satisfaction rating
for a meal?

....

....

....

....

A Mindful Meal

While there have been snippets of what mindful eating can look like throughout this workbook, the following is an example of a mindful meal. Note that your meals may be different from this example and from each other. It's not necessary to be *perfectly* mindful the entire meal to be considered engaging in a mindful eating practice.

Though this section focuses on when you eat the meal, the eating experience itself can be traced as far back as when you shop for your food. (See Mindful Meal Preparation on page 90.)

PREPARATION

You may find it helpful to create an environment that is conducive to being mindful and present. Here are a few ideas:

Designate an eating area. Try to keep it as clutter-free as possible.

Remove potential distractions. Turn off the TV and put away any reading material, phones, and tablets. You may play soft music in the background if you'd like.

Set the table. This helps provide a visual cue that the space is for eating. You may even want to lay out the fine china, set out a vase of flowers, and light a few candles for an extra-special meal.

SLOWING DOWN

Once you're seated at the table, ground yourself by taking a few deep breaths. This might be an opportunity for you to check in on what types of hunger are showing up for you and how hungry you are. If it's in your religious or spiritual tradition, you may want to say a prayer or blessing as a way to "press pause" while expressing thanks for the meal ahead.

As mentioned in previous chapters, you don't need to eat slowly to eat mindfully. However, slowing the pace of your eating can make it easier to be present and notice the nuances of what you experience throughout your meal.

SIGHT

As the saying goes, we eat with our eyes first. Our eyes can give us information about the color, shape, and texture of a food, as well as the amount available. Notice how the presentation of the food affects your appetite or desire to eat it, if at all. Our eyes also allow us to observe the environment around us. Notice how the lighting and décor of the room and how the table is set affects your eating experience.

SMELL

The smell of a food can help you get an idea of what it might taste like. Hot foods typically generate more aromas than foods that are served cold or at room temperature, so you may need to hold the food closer to your nose in order to smell it.

You may also notice how other smells around you—candles at the table, scented products being worn by your dining companions, or other foods being cooked and served at a restaurant, for example—intermingle with your food and change your eating experience.

As you eat, you will continue "smelling" the food through your nasal cavity, a phenomenon called *retronasal smell*. This affects how the flavor of the food is perceived. To experience retronasal smell, try this:

Plug your nose with one hand as you take a bite of food. As you chew the food, allow it to roll around your tongue and notice how it tastes. You'll likely notice that the flavor is subtler. After a few chews, unplug your nose. As the air starts to flow through your nasal cavity again, your sense of retronasal smell will become stronger, allowing you to experience more flavor from the food.

SENSATION

With finger foods, you can feel the texture and temperature of the food with your hands, but for the most part, in eating we rely on the nerve endings in our mouth and tongue for sensation. With each bite, notice how the sensations you get from the food changes as you chew and swallow.

You can also use your sense of touch to notice the environment around you: how the utensils feel in your hand, the cup as you raise it to your lips for a drink, or the texture of the napkin.

You may be surprised to learn that spicy foods activate our sense of touch, not taste. Capsaicin, the compound that makes spicy foods spicy, is actually an irritant, which is why we get that tingling, "burning" feeling when we eat spicy foods.

TASTE

Taste is usually the sense we think of when it comes to food and eating, yet as you've read thus far, all our senses contribute to the eating experience. While most of our taste buds are located on our tongue, there are some in the roof, sides, and back of the mouth, as well as in the throat. Our taste buds can detect five basic tastes: sweet, salty, sour, bitter, and umami/savory. The unique flavors we get from eating different foods are the result of the overlapping of these basic tastes, coupled with smell.

With each bite, notice how the taste of the food changes as you chew and swallow. You may also notice that as you become fuller, the taste of the food changes and becomes less enticing.

HEARING

Aside from crispy or crunchy foods, most of the foods we eat don't produce many sounds. In most Western cultures, we are discouraged from making sounds while we eat. By contrast, in some Asian cultures, chewing with the mouth open is not seen as taboo, and slurping noodles or tea is actually encouraged as a sign of appreciation. (Not only does slurping help cool the hot tea or broth, it's also thought to enhance the taste of the food by incorporating more airflow.)

Interestingly, in mindfulness, we often tune in to the sense of hearing first to capture information from our environment. As you eat, notice what happens when you focus on the sounds around you and from you. Perhaps you'll hear the tinkling of utensils on the plate, the hum of a fan or heater, the sound of food crunching between your teeth, or the conversation going on around you.

LEAVING A LITTLE BEHIND

Like slowing down, this is not a requirement of mindful eating, but eating with the intention to leave a few bites behind (even if you eventually end up deciding to eat it all) can help you be more present in your internal cues of fullness instead of the external cue of an empty plate.

Throughout the meal, check in with your hunger and fullness cues to see if you would like more. Some people find that having an external reminder, like putting your fork down every few bites, is helpful.

As you near the end of the meal, notice what the thought of leaving a few bites on your plate feels like. Does it feel reasonable or even necessary? Or does it feel uncomfortable? As a lifelong member of the "clean plate club," this is something I often struggle with myself because I worry about being wasteful. Others might worry that if they don't finish everything, they'll be hungry before the next meal.

We can't always predict how much food we want or need at the start of a meal. You may find it helpful to save the last bites in a container for later, as it can address any concerns you might have about food waste or feeling hungry sooner.

EXERCISE: REFLECTING ON YOUR MINDFUL MEAL

Use the suggestions in the previous section and the skills you have learned throughout this book to help guide you through a mindful meal. Once you are finished, respond to the following questions to help you reflect on your experience.

How did you feel before the meal? What sensations did you feel in your body? What thoughts and feelings were going through your mind?

....

....

....

....

....

As you ate your meal, did you struggle with staying mindful throughout? What were some strategies you used to help bring you back to the present?

....

....

....

....

What, if anything, did you notice that was different about your meal or your eating experience that you might not have noticed with similar meals in the past?

....

....

....

....

What, if anything, from your mindful meal would you take to future experiences?

....

....

....

What, if anything, from the experience would you like to let go of?

....

....

....

What, if anything, would you do differently at your next mindful eating practice?

....

....

....

Value Judgments

One of the key principles of mindfulness and mindful eating is nonjudgment. Our society's relationship with food and eating, however, is full of different forms of judgment. We judge foods not just on how they taste but also on their nutritional value, how they're prepared, how they're produced, how much they cost, and so on. It can be difficult to let go of our many opinions on food and eating and be present in the eating experience as a neutral observer.

"GOOD" FOOD VERSUS "BAD" FOOD

Healthy versus unhealthy. Clean versus processed. Superfood versus junk food. Always versus sometimes. Guilt-free versus indulgence. These are all just euphemisms for the way we assign moral value to food, which is usually based on what we perceive as its nutritional value.

MINDFUL MEAL PREPARATION

One of the reasons many people like cooking is because it can be a very tactile and engaging experience. Creating something from scratch can feel rewarding, and it is the perfect opportunity to infuse a mindfulness practice into the day. In addition to my Four Mindfulness Practice Principles (see page 7), here are some ideas to help you engage your senses the next time you are in the kitchen:

Invite yourself to use all of your senses as you interact with each ingredient. If possible, hold and feel each ingredient in your hand as you take it out of the fridge or pantry. Take the time to look at its color, size, shape, and texture. Use your sense of smell, and if appropriate, taste it, to make a note of how each component adds to your dish. (Your senses are also helpful in making sure nothing has spoiled!)

Use your hands as much as possible. What is it like to knead dough by hand instead of with a stand mixer or to toss a salad with your hands instead of a set of tongs? Of course, be aware of food safety (and your own safety!) when you try this tip.

Embrace change. What makes cooking seem so magical sometimes is the way different ingredients come together to make a dish. Notice how the raw ingredients transform throughout the cooking process.

We've been taught that to be healthy, we should eat more "good" foods, and fewer "bad" foods. Aside from the fact that no one seems to agree on what is good or bad (with the increasing popularity of the carnivore diet, even vegetables aren't always considered good anymore), this exaggerates the impact that individual behaviors actually have on health. The Centers for Disease Control and Prevention (CDC) estimates that only about 20 percent of our health is determined by our behaviors, with the vast majority of our health determined by social determinants such as socioeconomic status, education, and access to health care.

To make matters worse, not only do we assign moral value to food, we assign moral value to people who eat certain things or in a certain way. Think of how casually we say how "bad" we're being when we order dessert at the end of a meal, or click "like" on a social media post of a green smoothie or a salad?

What would it be like to give yourself permission to eat whatever you want, whenever you want? What would it be like to truly believe that all foods are good foods?

NONJUDGMENTAL LANGUAGE

Sometimes it may feel difficult to describe our eating experience in a nonjudgmental way. Even words like "delicious" or "scrumptious" are technically passing judgment on the taste of the food. It can be easier to shift to a nonjudgmental mind-set when you have the language to describe your experience. Here are some ideas you might find helpful:

Imagine yourself as a food critic. Wait, don't food critics *judge* restaurants? This may be true, but a review that simply says, "10/10. Delicious," isn't helpful to anyone. A good restaurant review transports the reader to the restaurant itself, setting the scene, describing the food, and telling all the stories behind it. The next time you eat, put yourself in the shoes of the critic: How would you describe your experience to others (before you get to the star rating)?

Pleasant, unpleasant, neutral. You may recognize this wording from the Hunger-Fullness Scale on page 38. Some people find this a helpful frame because instead of describing the food, you are describing how you feel after eating it. Though we typically associate "pleasant" with "good," and "unpleasant" with "bad," try to challenge yourself to let go of those associations. What if pleasant is just pleasant and unpleasant is just unpleasant? Can pleasant ever be bad or unpleasant ever be good?

Describing discomfort. Whenever you're unsure of how to describe a feeling, you might want to try on "discomfort" or "uncomfortable," then expand from there. What about the feeling is uncomfortable? Where is it located in your body? What is it like to try to sit with the discomfort instead of stuffing it down or trying to make it go away?

PERMISSION TO EAT

When I first met my client Natalie, she described herself as someone who took time and care in preparing balanced meals, yet struggled with snacking. Natalie noticed that she would often get hungry in the late afternoon, and there were almost always sweets in the break room at work. While her coworkers seemed to be satisfied with one or two cookies or candies, Natalie often found herself eating handfuls. At home, Natalie tried to manage the situation by not buying any treats, particularly chocolate and peanut butter, which were her favorites. However, she often found herself "scavenging" through her kitchen late at night, looking for something to eat.

Natalie and I spoke about giving herself permission to have snacks, particularly chocolate and peanut butter. While the knee-jerk reaction of many people is to think that they will "just eat junk food all the time," Natalie was able to see that this was a strategy that could work. Even though she didn't plan to have snacks in the afternoon and evening, she was practically eating every day at those times; planning would allow her to make different, more satisfying choices. She was also able to see that by giving herself permission to have treats, it was actually easier to say no. Instead of eating with a subconscious "last supper" mentality, she knew the treats would always be available if she wanted them.

The Role of Nutrition

Our approach to nutrition is often in the future tense. "Healthy" foods are ones that are meant to help us prevent disease, live longer, and lose weight (though I've already written ad nauseam about how that is unrelated to health and is incompatible with mindful eating). So where does nutrition fit with mindful eating, if at all?

One thing we can turn our attention to is how foods make us feel in the present moment and how we can use that knowledge to think about future meals. Often when we think of what we *want* to eat, we think of our mouth hunger. To me, good nutrition means we are using all the types of hunger to guide our food choices (see page 30).

Yes, we want our food to taste good; at the same time, our stomach hunger is searching for something that will provide energy and a feeling of fullness. Our brain hunger might be seeking certain nutrients or food that it knows from past experience will make us feel energized. Our heart hunger will want something that is satisfying and makes us feel good.

> Good nutrition is when we use all the types
> of hunger to guide our food choices.

STEPPING OFF THE SCALE

Many use a scale as a way to measure how well they're doing in terms of their health and their eating. Yet I've seen firsthand many clients who are "doing it right" in terms of eating balanced meals, staying hydrated, engaging in regular physical activity, keeping meticulous food records, and so on, only to have their weight stay the same or even increase. As a dietitian, I was taught that in these cases I was supposed to play detective: Were they measuring or weighing every morsel of food that passed through their lips? Were they writing down every time they tasted their food as they were cooking or cleaning off their kids' plates? Basically, I was supposed to figure out where my clients were (usually inadvertently) lying.

Because of factors like genetics, metabolism, aging, etc., even if every person on this planet ate the exact same meals every single day, we would not be the same size and shape. The scale only measures your weight, full stop. Don't let it try to tell you anything about your eating habits or your health. More important, it doesn't say anything about your worth or how the rest of your day should go after you step off of it.

If you weigh yourself regularly—even if it's just once a week—ask yourself what you have been letting the scale tell you. What would it be like if you put away the scale for an extended period or threw it out altogether?

THE HEALTH AT EVERY SIZE APPROACH

Our conventional approach to health and nutrition is considered "weight-centric," in that it deems certain body sizes to be unhealthy and considers achieving and maintaining a "healthy" body weight as a necessary part of health. On the other hand, Health At Every Size (HAES®) is a weight-neutral approach to health that proposes that all people are able to pursue health regardless of weight and rejects the use of weight, size, or BMI as proxies for health.

While HAES doesn't deny the correlation between body weight and certain health conditions, it questions the idea that weight is the *cause* of these conditions, considering the evidence that weight stigma is also correlated with poor health, regardless of body size. It also questions whether weight loss is an effective form of treatment, given that we currently don't have a safe and reliable method for people to lose weight and keep it off in the long term. The pursuit of weight loss is also independently correlated with weight cycling, disordered eating, and body-image concerns.

Despite the emphasis on size in its name, HAES practitioners and advocates seek to serve all marginalized identities, including people of color, queer identities, and disabled people, just to name a few.

HAES's guiding principles are weight inclusivity, health enhancement, respectful care, eating for well-being, and life-enhancing movement. As a dietitian, I generally work with clients in the area of "eating for well-being," and many are surprised to find that I don't give out meal plans or talk about weight loss. Instead, I use mindful eating and the HAES approach to help people attune to their own needs and figure out what good nutrition or healthy eating means for them as individuals, regardless of their current body size.

(Full disclosure: I am a member of the Association of Size Diversity and Health, the organization that owns and governs the HAES registered trademark.)

CULTIVATING HEALTHY EATING

Because I'm a dietitian, many people often assume that I'm all about helping people make "healthy" food choices and that anything food-related or eating-related that I talk about is *healthy*. I personally don't love using the word "healthy" as a descriptor because the definition of "health" is not universal and is often a moving target. No single food, meal, day, or even week of eating can make or break your health. Our health is dictated by a multitude of factors, including many that are outside of our control. I like to describe my work more as changing people's thoughts and behaviors around food and eating.

That being said, I respect that you might be motivated to use this workbook and try mindful eating in the pursuit of health. Mindful eating alone does not constitute healthy eating, nor do you need to be eating mindfully to eat healthfully. Though mindful eating and mindfulness already benefit health on their own, as discussed in chapter 1, combining them with other skills and strategies can make them powerful tools for health.

For example, you've learned how mindful eating can be a helpful tool in assessing how different foods affect your body. You may choose to combine this with a food/symptom journal to identify food sensitivities or with meal planning to help ensure you are choosing foods that make you feel good more often.

CULTIVATING SELF-CARE

Self-care is often mischaracterized as bubble baths and manicures. While those can be a part of self-care, a more accurate definition is "getting our needs met as best as we can." Mindfulness and mindful eating can be helpful in attuning to what those needs might be and sometimes are viewed as self-care in and of itself, as they provide an opportunity to slow down and be present in an otherwise fast-paced lifestyle.

Sometimes, self-care is easy; it presents us with a chance to slow down, unplug, and take a break. Other times, self-care requires effort, whether it's quieting those voices that tell you you're being selfish or dragging yourself outside because you know, deep down, that you'll feel better afterward. Sometimes, for whatever reason, your needs cannot be completely met. That's okay, too.

At the end of the day, self-care is about filling your own cup, whichever way you choose. It's about building resilience, so that you can continue to put your energy out into the world.

EXERCISE: THE LAST TIME YOU ATE

Use the following prompts to help you reflect on the last time you ate, and write your responses in the space provided. You may also choose to include the questions from the "Reflecting on Your Mindful Meal" exercise on page 87.

- When and where was the last time you ate?
- What made you decide to eat?
- What did you eat? (Describe it using all your senses: sight, smell, hearing, taste, and touch.)
- What thoughts and emotions came up as you were eating?
- What else was happening while you were eating (i.e., conversation, watching TV, reading, working, etc.)?
- How did you decide when to stop eating?
- What thoughts and emotions came up when you were finished eating?

....

....

....

....

Review the "Last Time You Ate" exercises on pages 14, 46, and 75. What are some similarities and differences between your eating experiences? How has putting together all the concepts in this workbook changed the way you eat, if at all?

....

....

....

Chapter Check-in

This chapter linked all the concepts discussed in this workbook to help you put together a "mindful meal." Hopefully you've had the opportunity to practice what you've learned so far. Remember there is no "right" or "wrong" way to eat mindfully—just keep my Four Mindfulness Practice Principles in mind (see page 7), and you are well on your way. As you continue to incorporate mindfulness and mindful eating into your daily routine, you will probably find elements that are more helpful for you; hold on to those elements and let go of any that aren't helpful.

What are some of your aha moments from this chapter? What are some areas you'd like to focus on as you continue to learn and build your practice?

....

....

....

....

....

....

CHAPTER FIVE

THE MINDFUL LIFESTYLE

One of the greatest benefits of mindful eating for me has been bringing the mind-set of nonjudgment and being present to other aspects of my life. It has allowed me to be a better practitioner for my clients and has also given me more space to practice self-compassion and self-care.

As you continue your mindful eating practice, you may find yourself— intentionally or unintentionally—bringing some of the concepts you've learned and practiced in this workbook into your daily life.

Learning and Unlearning

If you're freaking out because we're at the last chapter of this workbook and you're wondering why you don't get it yet, don't worry. Mindfulness and mindful eating aren't concepts that come naturally. Shifting our brain to become more mindful takes time and effort, so celebrate the concepts you have been able to integrate—even if you've only done them once.

In addition, some of the concepts we've discussed, like the Health At Every Size Approach on page 94, are downright radical. You might have noticed some feelings of anxiety or discomfort learning that the way we eat doesn't have as much impact on our weight or that our weight doesn't have as much impact on our health as we've been led to believe.

For most people, mindfulness and mindful eating don't simply come from reading a book. I invite you to not only revisit this workbook and the exercises but also seek out other resources and opportunities to practice mindful eating.

"In today's rush, we all think too much, seek too much, want too much and forget about the joy of just being."
—Eckhart Tolle

PLANNING FOR MINDFULNESS

On the surface, "planning" and "mindfulness" may seem like concepts that don't mix. Planning is about thinking about the future, while mindfulness is focused on the present. In our modern world, however, it is often helpful to use external cues as reminders to tune in. Planning ahead can help you make space for more opportunities to practice mindfulness. Here are some ideas to try:

- Set aside time to read and practice the exercises in this workbook, as well as to explore related resources.
- Plan your "mindful meals" ahead of time so you can set up a comfortable environment to practice mindful eating.
- Try a mindfulness bell app, like Lotus Bud or Mindfulness Bell on iOS or MindBell on Android, which can be set to ring randomly throughout the day as a reminder to "press pause and be present."

EXERCISE: BUILDING MINDFULNESS INTO YOUR DAY

Eating is not the only task in our daily lives that can easily become mindless. Have you ever walked or driven somewhere without really remembering how you even got there? Or noticed that your days are all so similar that they seem to blur together? There are many opportunities throughout the day to inject a little bit of mindfulness.

Choose a specific activity or length of time where you would like to practice mindfulness, and use my Four Mindfulness Practice Principles as a guide:

Press Pause and Be Present. Spend a few moments grounding yourself before you begin. Taking a few deep breaths can be a helpful reminder to be present and switch to a nonjudgmental mind-set.

Curiosity, Not Judgment. Approach the situation or activity as a neutral observer. Try to let go of past experiences you might have had and experience the moment as though you've never done it before.

Sensing, Not Slowing. Gather information about the experience using the senses of sight, smell, hearing, touch, and taste, as appropriate. In addition to observing the external environment, notice what physical sensations, thoughts, or emotions might be coming up for you as you engage in the activity or go about your day more mindfully.

Practice, Not Perfection. If this is new to you, you may notice some feelings of discomfort or awkwardness. While it may be tempting to judge yourself for them or try to make them go away, invite yourself to observe these feelings: What sensations are associated with these feelings? Where do they sit in your body? What is it like to sit with them instead of trying to change them?

REFLECTION

What activity or period of time did you choose? Why did you choose it?

....

....

....

....

What was it like to try to be more mindful for this activity or time period? Was it easy or difficult? What were some similarities and differences from times when you weren't purposefully mindful?

....

....

....

....

....

....

Would you try to be more mindful again in the future? Why or why not?

....

....

....

....

....

MINDFUL SHOPPING

We've discussed mindful eating and mindful meal preparation, so how about mindful grocery shopping? Don't laugh—I know the grocery store on weekends can be utter chaos, especially if you have kids in tow. Like the other mindfulness concepts discussed in this workbook, mindful shopping isn't necessarily about being zen; it's simply about engaging with the shopping experience in a more present and deliberate way.

In addition to my Four Mindfulness Practice Principles, try some of the following tips for a more mindful shopping experience:

Shop at off-peak hours. If possible, shop at a time when the store is less busy, like early in the morning or just before closing, and leave the kids at home if you can. This will help minimize distractions.

Use your senses to guide you. For many of us, the most mindful part of shopping is when we are selecting produce, using the senses of sight and touch to make sure we're not buying anything that is spoiled. Experiment with using the sense of smell when selecting produce or perhaps using more of your senses when choosing different foods.

Pay attention to the sounds of shopping. The clattering of shopping carts being wheeled down each aisle, the unmistakable beeps of the cash register, and the rustling of shopping bags are all unique to the experience of grocery shopping, yet are often relegated to background noise. While shopping, take a moment to notice the sounds around you. What do you hear?

Notice how you decide what to buy. Are you someone who writes a list and sticks to it? Or do you shop based on how you feel? What about if something is on sale? As you scan the items in your cart or basket, notice the different factors that influenced what you decided to purchase.

Beyond Food

For many of us, food is plentiful and easily accessible, making it a convenient answer to many different situations.

- Crying child? Soothe them with candy.
- First date? Make a dinner reservation.
- Bored? Peek inside the fridge.

While there is absolutely nothing wrong with turning to food in those situations, having alternate responses or solutions can be helpful. In fact, sometimes overreliance on food can keep us from finding answers that allow us to get to the heart of the issue.

- Crying child? Ask them what's wrong.
- First date? Try a new activity.
- Bored? Find something to do.

These examples are not here to say that one answer is better than the other. All answers are valid, and it may take some experimenting to find out which answers are the best for you.

Brain and Heart Hunger

As discussed, we are often told that we shouldn't eat when we're not physically hungry. Emotional eating is seen as a negative behavior we should try to avoid or stop. Allow me to repeat that there is nothing wrong with eating when you're not hungry or to soothe uncomfortable emotions. When other supports are unavailable, eating may be the best form of self-care.

What's unique about brain and heart hunger is that they can be satisfied without food. Sometimes when we experience brain and heart hunger, it's really signaling a deeper issue that needs to be addressed, and turning to food will only provide temporary relief. The following exercise will help you explore alternate responses to your brain and heart hunger.

EXERCISE: FEEDING YOUR BRAIN AND
HEART HUNGER WITHOUT USING FOOD

This exercise is most effective if you are experiencing brain or heart hunger without stomach hunger. For practice, you can refer back to situations that you recorded in the "Why Am I Hungry?" exercise on page 32, if appropriate.

Describe what was happening when you first started noticing the brain or heart hunger, paying attention to what might be a potential trigger. Was it a specific event? Place? Time of day?

....

....

....

Take a few deep breaths and allow yourself to do a quick body scan (see page 28). Where do you notice sensation, if any, in your body? What does it feel like?

....

....

....

Using the answers in the first two questions, try to name the emotions or thoughts that you feel are driving your brain or heart hunger. If you're feeling stuck, try the word "discomfort" or "uncomfortable" to see if it might be a good fit.

....

Ask yourself what you can do to address this thought or emotion without turning to food. The following list offers some ideas or you can add your own in the spaces provided.

Distractions	Support	Sit with and Address Feelings	Self-Care/Nurturing
Browse the internet and/or social media	Talk to, call, text, or email . . .	Journal	Schedule some "me time"
Color	A family member	Use RAIN and the CBT-based thought record to identify and reframe thoughts (page 70)	"Unplug" from technology
Do a puzzle	A close friend		Meditate
Do chores	A spiritual leader		Practice gratitude
Exercise	A therapist or other health professional	Urge surfing (page 52)	Practice self-compassion
Go outside		Address the situation that is triggering your emotions	Engage in a hobby you enjoy
Listen to music	Call a helpline		
Make a craft	Post on an online support group		Take a bath
Play a game on your phone		Get appropriate support	Take a nap/rest
Read	_____	_____	Buy yourself a small, non-food gift
Watch funny videos online	_____	_____	Book a spa day
Watch TV	_____	_____	
_____		_____	_____
_____			_____
			_____

It may be helpful to note which responses work best in different situations, keeping in mind that this may not be effective 100 percent of the time. Also, if you try one of these activities and still decide to eat, you're not doing anything wrong. In fact, when you're struggling to name what's behind your brain or heart hunger, sometimes choosing to eat mindfully and paying attention to how your body responds can give you more clues.

MINDFUL MOVEMENT

Many studies show that physical activity can help boost mood and relieve stress, in addition to its other health benefits. Unfortunately, like our relationship with food, diet culture has warped our relationship with exercise. Instead of seeing movement as something joyful on its own, exercise is often framed as a way to burn fat and calories and change our body size and shape. The "no pain, no gain" mind-set is encouraged, and gentle activities of short duration are disregarded. As a result, many of us view physical activity as an act of punishment instead of an act of self-care.

If you're curious about incorporating movement as a form of self-care, and it's been a while since you've engaged in physical activity, first talk with your doctor to determine if you have any activity restrictions. Next, consider what would make movement joyful for you. Perhaps it's the sense of accomplishment you get from lifting weights, completing a hike, or winning a competition, or the sense of camaraderie you get from a group class or playing a team sport. Maybe you like moving to music on the dance floor or in an exercise class, or perhaps you want to get back to an activity you enjoyed in the past.

Everything counts, even if it's stretching in your chair in the middle of a busy workday or regular daily movements like getting groceries or doing the laundry. Invite yourself to inject a bit of mindfulness into your movements, and count the benefits rather than calories burned.

It's Okay to Set Boundaries

Setting boundaries is a self-care skill that many people (myself included) often struggle with. We worry about hurting others' feelings or being seen as inflexible or selfish. In fact, most people find that setting and enforcing boundaries that align with their own values can actually strengthen their relationships with others, not push people away.

For example, if having alone time to recharge is important to you, setting and enforcing that boundary with your friends and family allows you to have the opportunity for self-care and "pour from a full cup," as opposed to feeling drained or resentful that you don't have time for yourself.

RECLAIMING YOUR RELATIONSHIP WITH FOOD

What does it mean to be in a relationship with food? Your relationship with food is really about how you feel about food and how food makes you feel. Given that our thoughts, feelings, and behaviors are connected, our relationship with food does affect our eating habits.

One of the telltale signs of a dysfunctional relationship with food is if you find yourself thinking about food *all the time*. It doesn't help that we're constantly inundated with conflicting messages about food, whether it's sensationalized health news, marketing and advertising, or "food porn" on social media.

Mindful eating is one of many tools that can help you reclaim your relationship with food by allowing you to observe the eating experience neutrally and without judgment. It reminds you that you are not your thoughts. When you're able to take food off the pedestal that society has built for it, it frees up your brain space for bigger, better things.

PERMISSION TO EAT DOESN'T MEAN YOU *HAVE* TO EAT

Earlier in this workbook, you learned that accepting your cravings and working toward giving yourself permission to eat all foods, using the concept of habituation, can help take the power and emotional charge away from food and give it back to you. This in turn helps you build trust in your body's ability to tell you what, how much, and when to eat, instead of relying on external cues and advice.

Often the source of anxiety around this idea comes from forgetting that having permission to do something doesn't mean that you *have* to do it. **You have the power to say no.** However, I invite you to explore the reasons behind choosing not to eat. Is it because you're not hungry or the food doesn't appeal to you? Or is it because of a belief that the food is "bad" or unhealthy?

EATING OUT

Eating away from home can seem challenging from a mindful eating perspective, especially if you are used to practicing mindful eating alone in your home environment. There are a lot more stimuli, distractions, and interruptions when eating out, and less control over the overall experience. Still, my Four Mindfulness Practice Principles (see page 7) can apply wherever you are and make it easier for you to tune in to your own needs, even at a busy restaurant. Here are some additional points you may consider when dining out:

More, or less: Some enjoy the additional stimuli that come with eating out, as it is like a playground for the senses. You can flit from taking in the décor to listening to the sounds around you to smelling the different dishes as they pass by your table, all before the server has even taken your order. Others are simply overwhelmed by this sensory overload. If that's the case for you, allow yourself to focus on just one sense at a time or one specific aspect of the dining experience, like the food, the conversation, or your own thoughts and feelings.

Compare and contrast: It's easy for some people to fall into "all-or-nothing" thinking when it comes to dining out. They will avoid restaurants because they think there's nothing "healthy" on the menu, but when they do go out, they go all out, choosing foods for the sake of being rebellious as opposed to ordering what they really want. Instead of perceiving dining out as a barrier to mindful eating, think of it as an invitation to notice, without judgment, the similarities and differences with eating in your home environment. You may also want to make note of what it is like to eat out mindfully, compared to past dining experiences.

Get curious: Restaurants are often set up to get diners to eat more and spend more money. Notice all the different drivers to eat that are different from your home environment. Some examples include larger portions, social eating, or the desire to get the most value for your money. Remember that this exercise in curiosity is not about looking for what might be wrong with restaurants or going to them. It's about observing without judgment.

EXERCISE: THE LAST TIME YOU ATE

Use the following prompts to help you reflect on the last time you ate, and write your responses in the space provided. Based on what you've learned in this chapter, you may want to choose to reflect on a meal you ate outside the home or however it would be most helpful for you.

- When and where was the last time you ate?
- What made you decide to eat?
- How did you feel before eating? What sensations did you feel in your body? What thoughts and feelings were going through your mind?
- What did you eat? (Describe it using all your senses: sight, smell, hearing, taste, and touch.)
- What thoughts and emotions came up as you were eating?
- What else was happening while you were eating (i.e., conversation, watching TV, reading, working, etc.)?
- If you were trying to eat mindfully, did you struggle with staying mindful throughout your meal? If so, what were some strategies you used to help bring you back to the present?
- How did you decide when to stop eating?
- What thoughts and emotions came up when you were finished eating?

....

....

....

....

....

....

Review the "Last Time You Ate" exercises on pages 14, 46, 75, and 96. What are some similarities and differences between your eating experiences? How has practicing mindfulness in other areas of your life changed the way you eat, if at all?

....

....

....

....

....

....

Making It a Family Matter

Having the support of your family can be helpful in your own mindful eating practice. For children, eating more mindfully can also set up a more positive relationship with food and eating into adulthood.

Using the five senses and attuning to hunger and fullness cues are good places to start introducing mindful eating to children. Ellyn Satter is a dietitian who specializes in family feeding dynamics. She created the concept of Division of Responsibilities, which places the responsibility of when, where, and what to eat on the caregivers and the responsibility of whether and how much to eat on the child. Instead of coaxing, bribing, or forcing the child to "clean their plate," it's about trusting that the child will meet their needs when they are eating according to their internal cues when a variety of nutritious choices is provided.

For some families, transitioning to eating more mindfully can be difficult, and it can be tempting to beat yourself up for not introducing the concepts sooner. All parents are doing the best they can with the knowledge and resources they have, and it's never too late to make changes, even if it's in very small steps.

ASKING FOR SUPPORT

Whether this workbook has been your first introduction to mindful eating or just one of many resources you have accessed, it never hurts to get more support. If you have friends or family members who are practicing mindful eating, you can make the experience more interactive and personal together.

There are also many mindful eating groups and forums online. The Center for Mindful Eating is an excellent resource (see the Resources section on page 161). You may also find it helpful to reach out to a healthcare professional, like a psychologist or a dietitian, who specializes in mindfulness or mindful eating, especially if you have medical concerns. They will be able to help you adapt the concepts of mindfulness and mindful eating to your health needs.

Spreading Mindfulness

As with any habit change, adopting a mindful eating practice can be easier when you have support from others. Alternately, perhaps you've already noticed some positive outcomes from mindful eating and would like others to experience those same benefits. There are a few things to keep in mind:

MEETING PEOPLE WHERE THEY ARE

Regardless of your intent, it's important to consider whether the other person is ready to receive the messages you are sharing. The idea is not to "convert" people. Anyone who decides to start a mindful eating practice has their own reasons for doing so, and not everyone will adopt it the same way you have.

You've probably experienced, at some point, a pushy salesperson trying to sell you something you didn't want or need, and it likely made you want to reject whatever they were selling even more. In the same way, you'll want to avoid being pushy, but you can still share information about mindful eating with a loved one who isn't ready to adopt the practice. It just means there are more steps to take for the message to land:

Ask for permission: It may seem awkward or like you're "giving up power" to ask for permission to talk about something, but it shows that you respect the person you're talking to and can pique their interest as well. You might start your conversation by saying something like:

- "I want to talk about something that is really important to me. Is it okay if I share that with you?"
- "It really hurts me to see you struggling, and I have some ideas that might be helpful. Is it all right if I share that with you?"
- "I have something that's been really helpful for my own relationship with food. Would you be interested in hearing about it?"

If their answer is yes, great, but if they say no, respect their choice. A mistake I often made in the past was to try to slide my point in even if they refused, which defeats the purpose of asking for permission in the first place. It's okay if people are not ready to start the conversation on mindful eating, and some people may never be open to hearing it. When that is the case, simply continue to live in your truth, and perhaps when others see the changes that are happening for you, they may be open to learning more.

Focus on awareness: When we share something we care deeply about, it makes sense that we want the other person to embrace it, as we have. In reality, it's rare for people to jump from not knowing about something to embracing it and adopting it right away. Looking back, you were probably skeptical and did a lot of your own research before deciding to implement mindful eating into your own life.

With that in mind, for many people, simply planting a seed and showing them that there is another way is enough. Most people will need to hear the same message many times over before they decide that it's something they want to pursue, if at all.

Speak to their values: Try to adapt what you share about mindful eating to what the other person cares about. For example, someone who values science might be more interested in hearing about the research on mindful eating, as opposed to your own experience, whereas someone who likes more practical information would be less interested to hear about the data and more about the "how to."

Be the change you want to see: It may sound cliché, but actions do speak louder than words. Starting a mindful eating practice not only has direct benefits for you, but you will also be sharing it with the world in a way that words probably can't express.

A MINDFUL MEALTIME WITH COMPANY

One way to introduce mindful eating to your friends and family is by making it interactive. The next time you are sharing a snack or a meal (particularly if it's something you haven't eaten before), invite everyone to eat it mindfully, perhaps using the "A Taste of Mindful Eating" exercise on page 23 as a guide.

You may also choose to gently introduce my Four Mindfulness Practice Principles through the mealtime conversation.

Press Pause and Be Present: You may want to begin the meal by inviting everyone to practice this principle with you. If you're worried about being too intrusive or sounding too spiritual, some socially acceptable ways of doing this might be to invite everyone to put their phone away, proposing a toast, or simply expressing gratitude for the meal and for everyone's presence.

Sensing, Not Slowing: Throughout the meal, check in with people on how the food tastes and how people are feeling. If someone is talking about past or future events, you may want to ask, "How do you feel about that now?" or, "What are your thoughts about that now?"

Curiosity, Not Judgment: Value judgments about food, bodies, and/or health are popular mealtime topics for some people. You may want to gently invite people to question some of these judgments by being curious by asking questions like, "What makes you say that?" or, "This dessert tastes delicious to me. What don't you like about it?"

As you are working on removing your own value judgments from the eating experience, you may find that hearing judgmental comments from others is upsetting or triggering. In that case, there's nothing wrong with setting a boundary around this. You may want to respond to comments by saying, "It makes me uncomfortable to talk about this right now. How about we talk about something else?" It might be helpful to keep some topics in mind to make this switch go more smoothly.

Practice, Not Perfection: Remember that everyone is at a different point when it comes to knowing what mindful eating is, let alone accepting and integrating it into their own lifestyle. Accept that not everyone will embrace mindful eating, nor will introducing it to others always turn out the way you hope. Focus on your own practice and allow others to find their own way.

EXERCISE: LOVING-KINDNESS (METTĀ) MEDITATION

Since we are talking about sharing mindfulness and mindful eating with others, I thought we would end this chapter with a loving-kindness meditation. This meditation, which culminates in sending loving-kindness to all beings, is meant to counter ill will and a negative state of mind.

Though Jon Kabat-Zinn popularized mindfulness in a secular, science-based way, many modern mindfulness practitioners have gone back to meditation's Buddhist roots. *Mettā*, which translates to loving-kindness, or benevolence, is a core belief in Buddhism.

You may want to record yourself reading the following passage, allowing enough time to follow the instructions as you read, and then play it back so that you can stay present in the activity. Before you get started, choose or formulate the phrase(s) you will use. You may choose some of the following traditional phrases, use all of them as reflected in the following passage, or formulate a wish of your own choosing:

- May I be happy and free.
- May I be healthy and strong.
- May I be safe.
- May I be loved.

Settle comfortably in your seat. If you are sitting in a chair, place your feet flat on the ground. If you feel comfortable doing so, close your eyes. Take a few deep breaths, feeling the rise of your chest with each inhale, and the fall with each exhale. Continue to do so until you feel relaxed and grounded.

Begin by directing your attention to yourself. Breathe gently, and with each breath, recite the phrase or phrases you have chosen, either aloud or inwardly to yourself: *May I be happy and free. May I be healthy and strong. May I be safe. May I be loved.* Hold a hand to your heart as you recite these phrases, if you wish. Repeat for a few rounds of breath.

Now, picture with your mind's eye someone you love. It may be a family member, a partner, or a close friend. Direct your loving-kindness to your loved one, imagining they are receiving your wishes with each exhale. Again, you may choose to recite the phrases aloud or in your head: *May you be happy and free.*

May you be healthy and strong. May you be safe. May you be loved. Continue for a few rounds of breath, and repeat with any other loved ones as desired.

Next, shift your attention to a neutral person. It could be someone that you might have seen at the grocery store or on the bus—someone with whom you have no relationship or friendship. *May you be happy and free. May you be healthy and strong. May you be safe. May you be loved.* Continue for a few rounds of breath, and repeat with others as desired.

Think of someone in your life who is difficult or who you may be in conflict with. Direct your loving-kindness to this person: *May you be happy and free. May you be healthy and strong. May you be safe. May you be loved.* Continue for a few rounds of breath, and repeat with any other difficult people as desired.

Finally, think of all of the beings on this Earth, big and small. Send your wishes to all beings: *May you be happy and free. May you be healthy and strong. May you be safe. May you be loved.* Continue for as long as you need. When you're ready, end your meditation by shifting your attention back to your breath, and slowly blink your eyes open.

> "May all beings everywhere be happy and free, and may the thoughts, words and actions of my own life contribute in some way to that happiness, and to that freedom for all."
> —*Hindu prayer*

Growing Your Practice

Throughout this workbook, you've learned many ideas for integrating mindfulness and mindful eating into your everyday life. If you're feeling a little overwhelmed and not sure where to go from here, take a deep breath. Mindful eating is a practice, not a destination. There is no "right" or "wrong" way to practice.

You may want to start by asking yourself, "What's one small way I can incorporate mindfulness or mindful eating today?"

It could be remembering to "press pause" before a meal, using all your senses to observe a bite of food, or reading and doing the exercises in this workbook.

If you like to track your progress, at the end of each day, reflect on the question, "How did I practice mindfulness or mindful eating today?" Even if it's a one-line answer in a journal, calendar, or even a note on your phone, over time, you'll be able to look back and see the progress you've made.

Chapter Check-in

In this chapter, you learned some ideas for integrating mindfulness into your daily life beyond the dining room table, as well as sharing the concepts of mindful eating with others, whether it's for your own support or helping them build their own practice.

What are some of your aha moments from this chapter? What are some areas you'd like to focus on as you continue to learn and build your practice? As you finish this workbook, what are your next steps?

....

....

....

....

....

....

....

CONCLUSION

Thank you for choosing this workbook as a resource to help you increase your understanding of mindfulness and mindful eating, and build or grow your practices in these areas. I hope you will finish this workbook having learned something new, or at least were able to revisit a topic in a different light.

Remember that this is not the end, but a stepping-stone. I hope that I have inspired you to seek out further resources and knowledge on mindfulness, mindful eating, and/or some of the other topics I've touched on in this book. Of course, you can continue to come back and review the information and exercises in this workbook to discover some things you might have missed the first time around or to go a little deeper with others.

I wish you all the best in your mindful eating practice, and I hope that it will change the way you view the world in a similar way that it did for me.

APPENDIX:
BLANK WORKSHEETS

You can download copies of these worksheets at
CallistoMediaBooks.com/MindfulEating

EXERCISE: PAINTED PICTURE

Although the focus of mindful eating is on the present moment, sometimes it is helpful to look ahead to the future to provide some guidance on where we would like to go with our practice. Reflect on what made you decide to read this workbook using the following prompts and write your responses in the space provided:

- What are you hoping to learn?
- What would your life be like when you have a regular mindful eating practice? In other words, what would you see, do, have, and be?
- "Paint a picture" by describing a typical day in your future life with a regular mindful eating practice.

EXERCISE: MINDFUL EATING ASSESSMENT

This assessment is adapted from the 20-Item Italian Mindful Eating Question-naire created by psychologist and The Center for Mindful Eating board member Dr. Cecilia Clementi and colleagues. The original questionnaire assesses for **awareness** of how food affects how you feel and for **recognition** of hunger and fullness cues. This assessment includes additional questions concern-ing **nonjudgment**.

Answer yes or no for each statement. In some cases, you might feel you fall somewhere in the middle. If that's the case, read over the statement a few times, and answer according to how you would *usually* act most of the time.

Awareness

1. Before I eat, I take a moment to appreciate colors and smells of food.   Y   N

2. I notice when the food I eat affects my emotional state.   Y   N

3. I taste every bite of food I eat.   Y   N

4. I recognize when I am eating and not hungry.   Y   N

Recognition of Hunger/Fullness

5. I stop eating when I am full, even when it is something I love.   Y   N

6. I recognize when I feel hungry, as opposed to other sensations, like thirsty or bored.   Y   N

7. If there is extra food I like, I take a second helping even though I am full.   Y   N

8. I only allow myself to eat at set mealtimes and snack times, regardless of how I feel.   Y   N

Nonjudgment

9. I categorize foods into "good" or "bad," based on how healthy I think they are.   Y   N

10. I don't allow myself to eat certain foods (aside from allergens).   Y   N

11. I get upset with myself if I eat something unhealthy or if I eat too much.   Y   N

12. I strive to be a "perfect eater."   Y   N

SCORING

For questions 1 to 6, give yourself 1 point for every "yes." For questions 7 to 12, give yourself 1 point for every "no." Then tally up your points for each of the three sections and record them here:

Category	Score
Awareness	
Recognition of Hunger/Fullness	
Nonjudgment	
Total Score	

The highest total score is 12 with 4 points in each category. High scores in each category and overall indicate better mindful eating skills. Keep in mind that there are many people who practice mindful eating regularly and do not have a "perfect" score.

This assessment is for interest only, so it is not meant to diagnose anything. Instead, it provides you with awareness of where you are now with your mindful eating. You may choose to complete this assessment again after you finish this workbook to help you track your progress.

EXERCISE: STEP-BY-STEP GUIDE TO HABIT CHANGE

This guide can help you create a game plan to change or stop an existing habit that is no longer serving you. Though this book focuses on changing habits that may be keeping you from eating mindfully or building a mindfulness practice, you can use these steps for any habit you are trying to stop or change, like biting your fingernails or going to bed late. Note that the steps don't always happen in this order, and you might find yourself returning to certain steps throughout the process.

1. **Identify what needs changing**. If you already have a clear idea of a habit that you would like to focus on, skip this step. Otherwise, let's kick things off with a **brain dump**. Set a timer for 10 minutes and write down everything you *could* change. If the timer goes off and the page isn't filled, set it for another 5 minutes and keep going.

2. **Get to know your habit.** From your brain dump, choose one habit you would like to focus on changing or stopping.

....

3. **Describe this habit in more detail.** What are its triggers? Does this habit tend to happen at certain times? Does this habit show up differently in different situations? You may want to answer this question from memory or pay attention to this habit for a few days and jot down your observations.

....

....

....

....

4. **Create new habits.** Reflect back on the "Painted Picture" exercise on page 6. How will changing this habit move you toward your painted picture, if at all? What will it look like when you successfully change this habit? What will you see, do, have, and be?

....

....

....

....

5. What are some action steps you can take to move you toward your "Painted Picture"?

....

....

....

....

....

....

Review the action steps you just listed, and choose some you would like to try the next time you notice a trigger. Write them down in the space below.

OBSERVATION LOG

Using this worksheet, keep a log of your progress in changing or stopping your habit.

Date	Trigger (Describe the situation, thoughts, and emotions.)	Response	Notes (What went well? What might you do differently next time?)

EXERCISE: A TASTE OF MINDFUL EATING

Traditionally, this exercise is done with a raisin, but you may choose to do this activity with any finger food. You may want to record yourself reading the following passage, allowing enough time to follow the instructions as you read, and then play it back so that you can stay present in the activity.

Begin by placing the food in front of you, and settle comfortably in your seat. If you are sitting in a chair, place your feet flat on the ground. If you feel comfortable doing so, close your eyes. Take a few deep breaths, feeling the rise of your chest with each inhale and the fall with each exhale. Continue like this until you feel relaxed and grounded.

Open your eyes and look at the food in front of you. Approach the food with curiosity, as though you've never seen anything like it before. Notice the information your sense of sight is telling you about this food: its color, shape, size, and texture. Continue like this, without judgment.

Let's add the sense of touch. Pick up the food and notice how it feels in your hand. You may roll it between your fingers or place it in one hand, then the other. Notice what your sense of touch is telling you about this food—its texture, shape, and temperature. You may notice that your eyes are receiving new information as well. Continue like this, without judgment.

Hold the food up to your nose and inhale deeply. Notice the information your sense of smell is telling you about this food. The sense of taste is closely linked to the sense of smell. Can you guess what this food might taste like based on how it smells? Continue like this, without judgment.

Now, take a bite of the food, or if it's small enough, place it in your mouth. Without chewing, roll it around with your tongue for a few moments. Notice what your senses of taste, touch, and smell are telling you about this food.

As you slowly begin to chew your food, notice what the sense of hearing is telling you about this food. Notice any new information that is being received by your senses of taste, touch, and smell, if at all. Continue like this, without judgment, as you chew and swallow your food in your own time.

REFLECTION

What was it like to taste your food this way? How does this compare to the way you normally eat?

....

....

....

....

....

....

Based on this exercise, what are some changes you might make to your current eating habits to help you eat more mindfully?

....

....

....

....

....

EXERCISE: BASIC BODY SCAN

This mindfulness meditation is popular with beginners, as it scans through the different parts of your body, allowing you to continue to shift your focus throughout, instead of focusing on one thing for an extended period of time.

For this meditation, you will be scanning up the right side of the body, then down the left, spending the length of one or two breaths on each part of the body. You may find that you have a different sequence and/or pace that works better for you. As you reach the different parts of your body, resist the urge to lessen, change, or get rid of the sensations you may feel, and instead, just notice.

You may want to record yourself reading the following passage, allowing enough time to follow the instructions as you read, and then play it back so that you can stay present in the activity.

Sit or lie down for this meditation, whichever feels most comfortable. If you are sitting in a chair, place your feet flat on the ground. If you feel comfortable doing so, close your eyes. Take a few deep breaths, feeling the rise of your chest with each inhale and the fall with each exhale. Continue like this until you feel relaxed, grounded, and ready to begin.

Focus your attention on your right toes . . . right foot . . . right calf and shin . . . right knee . . . right thigh . . . right hip . . . abdomen . . . chest . . . right fingers . . . right hand . . . right forearm . . . right elbow . . . right upper arm . . . right shoulder . . . neck . . . throat . . . mouth . . . lips . . . nose . . . eyes . . . forehead . . . crown of the head . . . back of the head . . . nape of the neck . . . upper back . . . left shoulder . . . left upper arm . . . left elbow . . . left forearm . . . left hand . . . left fingers . . . lower back . . . left hip . . . buttocks . . . left thigh . . . left knee . . . left calf and shin . . . left foot . . . left toes . . .

Close the meditation with a few deep breaths. Feel your lungs fill with each inhale, and with each exhale, imagine that the air you took in is spreading to all the corners of your body.

If there is an area of your body that is demanding your attention, imagine yourself sending your breath there, and notice whether the sensation changes. Take as much time as you need to slowly come out of the meditation.

REFLECTION

Were there any particularly interesting sensations you noticed while completing the body scan? Describe the sensations and where you felt them in your body.

....

....

....

....

....

If you felt any discomfort, did you have the urge to lessen or change the sensation, or make it go away? What was it like to focus on noticing and observing the sensation as opposed to changing it?

....

....

....

....

....

Optional: A body scan can be a regular part of your mindfulness practice. Each time you complete a scan, you may want to take notes in a journal to compare and contrast your experiences.

EXERCISE: WHY AM I HUNGRY?

Because different types of hunger often overlap, it's sometimes difficult to tease them apart. You may feel brain *and* stomach hunger if you wake up craving bacon and eggs for breakfast. You may feel stomach *and* heart hunger after a stressful day at work with no breaks. The purpose of this exercise is not to point out that there is a right or wrong time to eat; rather, it's to highlight how complex hunger and appetite can be.

You may choose to complete this activity over the course of a day, or at times when you are eating outside of your regular meals and snacks.

Time	Place/ Situation	Type of Hunger				Body Sensations	Notes
		STOMACH	BRAIN	HEART	MOUTH		

REFLECTION

What type(s) of hunger tend to show up most often for you?

....

What are some of the similarities and differences between how the different types of hunger feel in your body?

....

....

....

....

How do the different types of hunger affect what or how much you eat, if at all?

....

....

....

....

EXERCISE: THE HUNGER-FULLNESS SCALE

Often when we talk about hunger and fullness, it is presented as a dichotomy: You're hungry or you're full. In reality, there is a spectrum of physical sensations that you may experience.

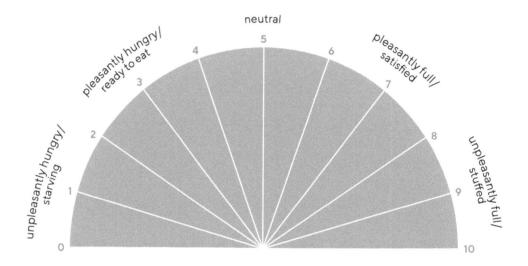

USING THE HUNGER-FULLNESS SCALE

Each person's hunger and fullness cues will be different. Use the Hunger-Fullness Scale as a guide. The next time you are about to eat, check in and ask yourself, "Where am I on the Hunger-Fullness Scale right now?"

Once you've decided, ask yourself, "How is my body telling me that I am at X on the Hunger-Fullness Scale?" Jot down some of the sensations you feel on the corresponding space on the scale. Repeat this at the end of your meal.

Continue this process over several days until you have a descriptor for each area of the scale. Doing this is not meant to change your eating habits or prevent you from eating; rather, it's to help you get into the practice of observing your hunger and fullness cues.

You will likely notice that many different factors contribute to your hunger and fullness. While you may reach a certain point of fullness from a meal on one day, you may have a completely different experience on another. Allow yourself to experiment and simply be curious without judgment.

REFLECTION

Once you become more familiar with your hunger and fullness cues, here are some questions to consider:

What are the similarities and differences between the different levels of hunger and fullness? Do some sensations only appear in certain cases?

....

....

What happens if you start eating at a lower point on the scale (i.e., hungrier) than you normally do? What if you start at a higher point (i.e., fuller)?

....

....

What happens if you stop eating at a lower point on the scale (i.e., hungrier) than you normally do? What if you stop at a higher point (i.e., fuller)?

....

....

How do different levels of hunger affect what and how much you eat, if at all?

....

....

EXERCISE: URGE SURFING

See the exercise on page 52. Describe and/or draw the physical sensation of your craving. Where was it located? What did it feel and/or look like?

How did your craving change as you continued to breathe, if at all?

....

....

....

....

....

How did you feel at the end of the meditation?

....

....

....

....

....

If at the end of this urge surfing activity, you still feel the urge to eat, **go ahead and eat**. Remember that **you didn't do anything wrong**. Sometimes a craving may last much longer or be more intense than you anticipated. Sometimes urge surfing just doesn't fit with your current situation. **The point is not to stop yourself from eating**. Instead, it's to use your cravings as an opportunity to get curious and practice responding to them in a different, more purposeful way.

EXERCISE: YOUR EMOTIONS IN COLOR

Get some different colored pens, markers, or pencils: things are about to get colorful! This activity will help you get a better sense of the physical sensations associated with your emotions.

1. Choose an emotion from the following list and circle it with a specific color, or write your own emotion in one of the spaces provided.
2. Using the same color, mark or circle the area of your body where you feel this emotion on the silhouette.
3. Using the same color, on the lines below the silhouette, describe specifics about the sensation (i.e., tingling, pressure, pain) and whether you feel the sensation is pleasant, unpleasant, or neutral.
4. Repeat with as many emotions and colors as you wish.

Happy	Sad	Angry	Bored	Stressed
Tired	Uncomfortable	Upset	Scared	Worried

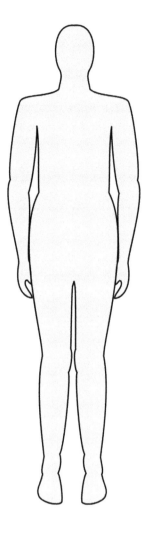

....

....

....

....

....

....

EXERCISE: HOW DO YOU FEEL WHEN YOU EAT?

This exercise will help you identify some of the factors that may be influencing your eating habits. You may fill out the following worksheet over the course of a day, or you may choose to only do this activity when you notice that you are eating emotionally.

REFLECTION

After reviewing your completed worksheet, what, if any, patterns or potential triggers do you notice?

....

....

....

....

....

Time	Location	How You Feel Before Eating	What You Ate	How You Feel During/After Eating	Pleasant/ Unpleasant/ Neutral	Additional Notes

EXERCISE: DISRUPTING THE EATING EXPERIENCE

Changing *how* you eat can take your brain out of eating on autopilot, which can help you be more aware and present in the experience. To get started, choose a disruption from the following list:

- Eating without any distractions
- Eating with your nondominant hand
- Eating something you usually eat with your hands (i.e., a sandwich or wrap) with a knife and fork
- Eating with a different eating utensil, such as eating soup with a fork
- Putting your eating utensil down between bites
- Chewing each bite at least 20 times before swallowing
- Eating dessert before your main course
- Plating your meal beforehand (if you normally serve your meals family-style)
- Serving your meals family-style (if you normally plate your meals before sitting at the table)
- Not finishing all the food on your plate

Begin your meal by grounding yourself with a few deep breaths. Approach your meal with curiosity, and as you eat your meal while engaging in the disruption you chose, notice, without judgment, the information you are receiving from your senses, thoughts, and emotions about your meal. You do not have to continue with your disruption for the entire meal.

REFLECTION

How did the disruption affect your eating experience, if at all?

....

....

....

Did the disruption help you eat more mindfully? Why or why not?

....

....

....

EXERCISE: CBT-BASED THOUGHT RECORD

In CBT, a thought record can help us become more aware of our negative thoughts so that we can find ways to shift them into more neutral or positive thoughts. You will notice that some of the steps overlap with mindfulness work.

Column 1: Acknowledge the situation/identify the trigger: When you notice a negative or unhelpful thought, make note of the situation. Ask yourself the five "Ws"—who, what, where, why, and when—to help you figure out what might have triggered these negative thoughts. (This step incorporates the "R" and "I" of RAIN.)

Column 2: Notice your physical and emotional feelings: What bodily sensations are coming up for you? What emotions are coming up for you? If it is helpful, you can rate the intensity of how you feel on a scale of 1 to 10. (This step also incorporates the "R" of RAIN.)

Column 3: Bring to mind the unhelpful thoughts and images: Often the mean-spirited voice in our head is not very creative and repeats the same phrases over and over again. Allow yourself to replay the tape one more time, so you can get those thoughts down on paper.

Columns 4 and 5: Just the facts: What are the facts that *support* your thought versus the facts that *don't support* them?

Colum 6: Respond to, or reframe, the thought: Given the facts, is your initial thought absolutely true? (Not likely.) How can you respond to your thought in a more reasonable and realistic way? How can you rephrase your thought so that it is more helpful?

Column 7: Reflection: Take note of your physical and emotional feelings again. How have things shifted, if at all?

THOUGHT RECORD

Situation/ Trigger	How do I feel physically and emotionally?	Unhelpful Thoughts/ Images	Facts that support my thoughts	Facts that don't support my thoughts	Respond or Reframe	Reflection (How do I feel physically and emotionally now?)

EXERCISE: HUNGER, FULLNESS, AND SATISFACTION TRACKER

Feeling full is different from feeling satisfied. As mentioned, there are many different parts of a meal that can make it more or less satisfying. For example, most people would probably choose a refreshing iced drink over a hot cocoa on a summer day.

The following tracker will help you continue to practice using the Hunger-Fullness Scale on page 38, as well as notice some of the different factors that play into making a meal satisfying.

Time	Hunger/Fullness Rating Before Eating	Food Eaten	Hunger/Fullness Rating After Eating	Satisfaction Rating	Notes

REFLECTION

What are some patterns you've noticed in your hunger, fullness, and/or satisfaction ratings, if any?

....

....

....

....

How did your hunger or fullness contribute to your satisfaction ratings, if at all?

....

....

....

....

What are some factors that tend to contribute to your satisfaction rating for a meal?

....

....

....

....

EXERCISE: REFLECTING ON YOUR MINDFUL MEAL

Use the suggestions in the previous section and the skills you have learned throughout this book to help guide you through a mindful meal. Once you are finished, respond to the following questions to help you reflect on your experience.

How did you feel before the meal? What sensations did you feel in your body? What thoughts and feelings were going through your mind?

....

....

....

....

....

As you ate your meal, did you struggle with staying mindful throughout? What were some strategies you used to help bring you back to the present?

....

....

....

....

What, if anything, did you notice that was different about your meal or your eating experience that you might not have noticed with similar meals in the past?

....

....

....

What, if anything, from your mindful meal would you take to future experiences?

....

....

....

What, if anything, from the experience would you like to let go of?

....

....

....

What, if anything, would you do differently at your next mindful eating practice?

....

....

....

EXERCISE: BUILDING MINDFULNESS INTO YOUR DAY

Eating is not the only task in our daily lives that can easily become mindless. Have you ever walked or driven somewhere without really remembering how you even got there? Or noticed that your days are all so similar that they seem to blur together? There are many opportunities throughout the day to inject a little bit of mindfulness.

Choose a specific activity or length of time where you would like to practice mindfulness, and use my Four Mindfulness Practice Principles as a guide:

Press Pause and Be Present. Spend a few moments grounding yourself before you begin. Taking a few deep breaths can be a helpful reminder to be present and switch to a nonjudgmental mind-set.

Curiosity, Not Judgment. Approach the situation or activity as a neutral observer. Try to let go of past experiences you might have had and experience the moment as though you've never done it before.

Sensing, Not Slowing. Gather information about the experience using the senses of sight, smell, hearing, touch, and taste, as appropriate. In addition to observing the external environment, notice what physical sensations, thoughts, or emotions might be coming up for you as you engage in the activity or go about your day more mindfully.

Practice, Not Perfection. If this is new to you, you may notice some feelings of discomfort or awkwardness. While it may be tempting to judge yourself for them or try to make them go away, invite yourself to observe these feelings: What sensations are associated with these feelings? Where do they sit in your body? What is it like to sit with them instead of trying to change them?

REFLECTION

What activity or period of time did you choose? Why did you choose it?

....

....

....

....

What was it like to try to be more mindful for this activity or time period? Was it easy or difficult? What were some similarities and differences from times when you weren't purposefully mindful?

....

....

....

....

....

....

Would you try to be more mindful again in the future? Why or why not?

....

....

....

....

EXERCISE: FEEDING YOUR BRAIN AND HEART HUNGER WITHOUT USING FOOD

This exercise is most effective if you are experiencing brain or heart hunger without stomach hunger. For practice, you can refer back to situations that you recorded in the "Why Am I Hungry?" exercise on page 32, if appropriate.

Describe what was happening when you first started noticing the brain or heart hunger, paying attention to what might be a potential trigger. Was it a specific event? Place? Time of day?

....

....

....

Take a few deep breaths and allow yourself to do a quick body scan (see page 28). Where do you notice sensation, if any, in your body? What does it feel like?

....

....

....

Using the answers in the first two questions, try to name the emotions or thoughts that you feel are driving your brain or heart hunger. If you're feeling stuck, try the word "discomfort" or "uncomfortable" to see if it might be a good fit.

....

Ask yourself what you can do to address this thought or emotion without turning to food. The following list offers some ideas or you can add your own in the spaces provided.

Distractions	Support	Sit with and Address Feelings	Self-Care/Nurturing
Browse the internet and/or social media	Talk to, call, text, or email . . .	Journal	Schedule some "me time"
Color	A family member	Use RAIN and the CBT-based thought record to identify and reframe thoughts (page 70)	"Unplug" from technology
Do a puzzle	A close friend		Meditate
Do chores	A spiritual leader		Practice gratitude
Exercise	A therapist or other health professional	Urge surfing (page 52)	Practice self-compassion
Go outside	Call a helpline	Address the situation that is triggering your emotions	Engage in a hobby you enjoy
Listen to music	Post on an online support group		Take a bath
Make a craft			
Play a game on your phone	_____	Get appropriate support	Take a nap/rest
Read	_____	_____	Buy yourself a small, non-food gift
Watch funny videos online	_____	_____	Book a spa day
Watch TV		_____	_____
_____			_____
_____			_____

It may be helpful to note which responses work best in different situations, keeping in mind that this may not be effective 100 percent of the time. Also, if you try one of these activities and still decide to eat, you're not doing anything wrong. In fact, when you're struggling to name what's behind your brain or heart hunger, sometimes choosing to eat mindfully and paying attention to how your body responds can give you more clues.

RESOURCES

Books

Body Kindness by Rebecca Scritchfield (Workman Publishing Company, 2016)

Body Respect by Linda Bacon and Lucy Aphramor (BenBella Books, 2014)

Child of Mine by Ellyn Satter (Bull Publishing Company, 2000)

The Core Concepts of Mindful Eating by Megrette Fletcher (Megrette Fletcher, 2017)

Eating in the Light of the Moon by Anita A. Johnston (Gurze Books, 2000)

Intuitive Eating by Evelyn Tribole and Elyse Resch (St. Martin's Griffin, 2012)

The Intuitive Eating Workbook by Evelyn Tribole and Elyse Resch (New Harbinger Publications, 2017)

Radical Acceptance by Tara Brach (Bantam, 2004)

Secrets of Feeding a Healthy Family by Ellyn Satter (Kelcy Press, 2008)

Websites

Association for Size Diversity and Health (www.sizediversityandhealth.org)

The Center for Mindful Eating (www.thecenterformindfuleating.org)

Intuitive Eating (www.intuitiveeating.org)

National Eating Disorders Association (www.nationaleatingdisorders.org) · Helpline: (800) 931-2237

REFERENCES

"4 Differences Between CBT and DBT and How to Tell Which Is Right for You." Skyland Trail. August 3, 2017. Accessed October 31, 2018. https://www .skylandtrail.org/About/Blog/ctl/ArticleView/mid/567/articleId/6747 /4-Differences-Between-CBT-and-DBT-and-How-to-Tell-Which-is-Right -for-You.

Allen, Micah, Martin Dietz, Karina S. Blair, Martijn van Beek, Geraint Rees, Peter Vestergaard-Poulsen, Antoine Lutz, and Andreas Roepstorff. "Cognitive-Affective Neural Plasticity Following Active-Controlled Mindfulness Intervention." *The Journal of Neuroscience* 32, no. 44 (October 2012): 15601–10. doi:10.1523 /JNEUROSCI.2957-12.2012.

American Academy of Pediatrics. "Physical Development: What's Normal? What's Not?" HealthyChildren.org. Last updated May 22, 2015. Accessed September 6, 2018. www.healthychildren.org/English/ages-stages/gradeschool /puberty/Pages/Physical-Development-Whats-Normal-Whats-Not.aspx.

American Psychiatric Association. *Diagnostic and Statistical Manual of Mental Disorders.* 5th ed. Washington, DC: American Psychiatric Association, 2013.

Association for Size Diversity and Health. "HAES® Principles: The Health at Every Size Approach." ASDAH: Association for Size Diversity and Health. Accessed August 11, 2018. www.sizediversityandhealth.org/content.asp?id=152.

Australian Government: National Health and Medical Research Council. "Clinical Practice Guidelines for the Management of Overweight and Obesity in Adults,

Adolescents and Children in Australia (2013)." NHMRC.gov.au. Accessed September 6, 2018. www.nhmrc.gov.au/guidelines-publications/n57.

Baer, Drake. "The Father of Mindfulness on What Mindfulness Has Become." *Thrive Global.* April 12, 2017. Accessed September 6, 2018. medium.com/thrive-global /the-father-of-mindfulness-on-what-mindfulness-has-become-ad649c8340cf.

Benzo, Roberto B., Janae L. Kirsch, and Carlie Nelson. "Compassion, Mindfulness, and the Happiness of Health Care Workers." *Explore (NY)* 13, no. 3 (May 2017): 201–6. doi:10.1016/j.explore.2017.02.001.

Berg, Jeremy M., John L. Tymoczko, and Lubert Stryer. *Biochemistry.* 5th ed. New York, NY: W. H. Freeman, 2002.

Binge Eating Disorder Association. "Binge Eating Disorder Causes and Risk Factors." Accessed September 2, 2018. https://bedaonline.com/understanding -binge-eating-disorder/binge-eating-disorder-causes/.

Bornemann, Boris, Beate M. Herbert, Wolf E. Mehling, and Tania Singer. "Differ-ential Changes in Self-Reported Aspects of Interoceptive Awareness Through 3 Months of Contemplative Training." *Frontiers in Psychology* 5 (January 2015): 1504. doi:10.3389/fpsyg.2014.01504.

Boyland, E. J., S. Nolan, B. Kelly, C. Tudur-Smith, A. Jones, J. C. Halford, and E. Robinson. "Advertising as a Cue to Consume: A Systematic Review and Meta-analysis of the Effects of Acute Exposure to Unhealthy Food and Nonalcoholic Beverage Advertising on Intake in Children and Adults." *The American Journal of Clinical Nutrition* 103, no. 2 (2016): 519-33. doi:10.3945 /ajcn.115.120022.

Brown, Kirk Warren, Robert J. Goodman, Richard M. Ryan, and Bhikku Anālayo. "Mindfulness Enhances Episodic Memory Performance: Evidence from a Multi-method Investigation." *PLOS One* 11, no. 4 (April 2016): e0153309. doi:10.1371 /journal.pone.0153309.

Canadian Mental Health Association, BC Division. "What's the Difference between CBT and DBT?" HereToHelp, 2015. Accessed October 31, 2018.

http://www.heretohelp.bc.ca/ask-us/whats-the-difference-between-cbt-and-dbt.

The Center for Mindful Eating. "Position on Mindful Eating & Weight Concerns." Last modified July 18, 2016. Accessed September 6, 2018. www.thecenterfor mindfuleating.org/Weight-concerns.

The Center for Mindful Eating. "The Principles of Mindful Eating." Last modified August 2013. Accessed July 19, 2018. www.thecenterformindfuleating.org /Principles-Mindful-Eating.

Clementi, Cecilia, Giulia Casu, and Paola Gremigni. "An Abbreviated Version of the Mindful Eating Questionnaire." *Journal of Nutrition Education and Behavior* 49, no. 4 (April 2017): 352–6.e1. doi:10.1016/j.jneb.2017.01.016.

Denny, Katherine G., and Hans Steiner. "External and Internal Factors Influencing Happiness in Elite Collegiate Athletes." *Child Psychiatry and Human Development* 40, no. 1 (March 2009): 55–72. doi:10.1007/s10578-008-0111-z.

Fletcher, Megrette. *Core Concepts of Mindful Eating: The Professional Edition.* Epping, NH: Megrette Fletcher, 2017.

Fothergill, Erin, Juen Guo, Lilian Howard, Jennifer C. Kerns, Nicolas D. Knuth, Robert Brychta, and Kong Y. Chen, et al. "Persistent Metabolic Adaptation 6 Years After 'The Biggest Loser' Competition."*Obesity (Silver Spring)* 24, no. 8 (August 2016): 1612–19. doi:10.1002/oby.21538.

Friedman, ScM, Roberta R., and Rebecca Puhl, PhD. *Weight Bias: A Social Justice Issue—A Policy Brief.* New Haven, CT: Yale Rudd Center for Food Policy & Obesity, 2012.

Harrison, Christy, MPH, RD, CDN (blog). "What is Diet Culture?" August 10, 2018. Accessed September 6, 2018. christyharrison.com/blog/what-is-diet-culture.

Hölzel, Britta K., James Carmody, Mark Vangel, Christina Congleton, Sita M. Yerramsetti, Tim Gard, and Sara W. Lazar. "Mindfulness Practice Leads to Increases in Regional Brain Gray Matter Density." *Psychiatry Research* 191, no. 1 (January 2011): 36–43. doi:10.1016/j.pscychresns.2010.08.006.

Hong, Phan Y., David A. Lishner, and Kim H. Han. "Mindfulness and Eating: An Experiment Examining the Effect of Mindful Raisin Eating on the Enjoyment of Sampled Food." *Mindfulness* 5, no. 1 (February 2014): 80–7. doi:10.1007/s12671-012-0154-x.

Hunger, Jeffery M., and Brenda Major. "Weight Stigma Mediates the Association Between BMI and Self-Reported Health."*eHealth Psychology* 34, no. 2 (February 2015): 172–5. doi: 10.1037/hea0000106.

Hunger, Jeffery M., Brenda Major, Alison Blodorn, and Carol T. Miller. "Weighed Down by Stigma: How Weight-Based Social Identity Threat Contributes to Weight Gain and Poor Health." *Social and Personality Psychology Compass* 9, no. 6 (June 2015): 255–68. doi:10.1111/spc3.12172.

Icahn School of Medicine at Mount Sinai. "Brain Rewards Pathways." Accessed August 8, 2018. labs.neuroscience.mssm.edu/brain-reward-pathways/.

Johnston, Anita A., PhD. *Eating in the Light of the Moon: How Women Can Transform Their Relationship with Food Through Myths, Metaphors, and Storytelling.* Carlsbad, CA: Gürze Books, 1996.

Khoury, Bassam, Manoj Sharma, Sarah E. Rush, and Claude Fournier. "Mindfulness-Based Stress Reduction for Healthy Individuals: A Meta-Analysis." *Journal of Psychosomatic Research* 78, no. 6 (June 2015): 519–28. doi:10.1016/j.jpsychores.2015.03.009.

Konturek, P.C., T. Brzozowski, and S.J. Konturek. "Stress and The Gut: Pathophysiology, Clinical Consequences, Diagnostic Approach and Treatment Options." *Journal of Physiology and Pharmacology* 62, no. 6 (December 2011): 591–9. www.ncbi.nlm.nih.gov/pubmed/22314561.

Light of the Moon Café (website). Accessed July 24, 2018. http://lightofthemooncafe.com.

Mann, Traci, A. Janet Tomiyama, Erika Westling, Ann-Marie Lew, Barbra Samuels, and Jason Chatman. Medicare's Search for Effective Obesity

Treatments: Diets Are Not the Answer." *American Psychologist* 62, no. 3 (April 2007): 220–33. doi:10.1037/0003-066X.62.3.220.

Martinez, Steven. "New Products." United States Department of Agriculture: Economic Research Service. Last modified April 5, 2017. Accessed September 6, 2018. www.ers.usda.gov/topics/food-markets-prices/processing-marketing /new-products/.

McKay, Sarah. "Neuroscience Insight: How to Break Bad Habits." The Chopra Center. Accessed July 20, 2018. chopra.com/articles/neuroscience-insight -how-to-break-bad-habits.

Miller, Carla K., Jean L. Kristeller, Amy Headings, Haikady Nagaraja, and W. Fred Miser. "Comparative Effectiveness of a Mindful Eating Intervention to a Diabetes Self-Management Intervention Among Adults with Type 2 Diabetes: A Pilot Study." *Journal of the Academy of Nutrition and Dietetics* 112, no. 11 (November 2012): 1835–42. doi:10.1016/j.jand.2012.07.036.

Mindful Staff. "Jon Kabat-Zinn: Defining Mindfulness." *Mindful.* January 11, 2017. Accessed September 6, 2018. www.mindful.org/jon-kabat-zinn-defining -mindfulness/.

Mindfulness.org.au. "Teaching Urge Surfing to Clients." Accessed July 24, 2018. www.mindfulness.org.au/teach-urge-surfing.

Mosley, Michael. "The Second Brain in Our Stomachs." *BBC TV.* July 11, 2012. Accessed September 6, 2018. www.bbc.com/news/health-18779997.

Mrazek, Michael D., Michael S. Franklin, Dawa Tarchin Phillips, Benjamin Baird, and Jonathan W. Schooler. "Mindfulness Training Improves Working Memory Capacity and GRE Performance While Reducing Mind Wandering." *Psychological Science* 24, no. 5 (May 2013): 776–81. doi:10.1177/0956797612459659.

National Center for HIV/AIDS, Viral Hepatitis, STD, and TB Prevention. "NCHH-STP Social Prevention." Last modified March 21, 2014. Accessed September 6, 2018. www.cdc.gov/nchhstp/socialdeterminants/faq.html.

National Eating Disorders Association. "NEDA: Feeding Hope." Accessed July 26, 2018. www.nationaleatingdisorders.org.

O'Leary, Karen, and Samantha Dockray. "The Effects of Two Novel Gratitude and Mindfulness Interventions on Well-Being." *The Journal of Alternative and Complementary Medicine* 21, no. 4 (April 2015): 243–5. doi:10.1089/acm.2014.0119.

Portland Psychotherapy Team. "Riding the Wave: Using Mindfulness to Cope with Urges." Portland Psychotherapy. Accessed July 24, 2018. portlandpsycho therapyclinic.com/2011/11/riding-wave-using-mindfulness-help-cope-urges/.

Proietto, Joseph. "Chemical Messengers: How Hormones Make Us Feel Hungry and Full." *The Conversation.* September 25, 2015. Accessed September 6, 2018. theconversation.com/chemical-messengers-how-hormones-make-us-feel -hungry-and-full-35545.

Resnick, Brian, and Julia Belluz. "A Top Cornell Food Researcher Has Had 13 Studies Retracted. That's a Lot." Vox. September 21, 2018. Accessed October 3, 2018. https://www.vox.com/science-and-health/2018/9/19/17879102/brian -wansink-cornell-food-brand-lab-retractions-jama.

Rodriguez Vega, Beatriz, Javier Melero-Llorente, Carmen Bayon Perez, Susana Cebolla, Jorge Mira, Carla Valverde, and Alberto Fernández-Liria. "Impact of Mindfulness Training on Attentional Control and Anger Regulation Processes for Psychotherapists in Training." *Psychotherapy Research* 24, no. 2 (2014): 202–13. doi:10.1080/10503307.2013.838651.

Russell-Williams, Jesse, Wafa Jaroudi, Tania Perich, Siobhan Hoscheidt, Mohamed El Haj, and Ahmed A. Moustafa. "Mindfulness and Meditation: Treating Cognitive Impairment and Reducing Stress in Dementia." *Reviews in the Neurosciences* (February 2018). doi:10.1515/revneuro-2017-0066.

Sanger, Gareth J., Per M. Hellström, and Erik Näslund. "The Hungry Stomach: Physiology, Disease, and Drug Development Opportunities." *Frontiers in Pharmacology* 1 (February 2011): 145. doi:10.3389/fphar.2010.00145.

Swaminathan, Nikhil. "Why Does the Brain Need So Much Power?: New Study Shows Why the Brain Drains So Much of the Body's Energy." *Scientific American.* April 29, 2008. Accessed September 6, 2018. www.scientificamerican.com /article/why-does-the-brain-need-s/.

Tara Brach (blog). "Blog: The RAIN of Self-Compassion." Accessed July 26, 2018. www.tarabrach.com/selfcompassion1/.

Taren, Adrienne A., Peter J. Gianaros, Carol M. Greco, Emily K. Lindsay, April Fairgrieve, Kirk Warren Brown, and Rhonda K. Rosen, et al. "Mindfulness Meditation Training Alters Stress-Related Amygdala Resting State Functional Connectivity: A Randomized Controlled Trial." *Social Cognitive and Affective Neuroscience* 10, no. 12 (December 2015): 1758–68. doi:10.1093/scan/nsv066.

Tribole, Evelyn, and Elyse Resch. *The Intuitive Eating Workbook: 10 Principles for Nourishing a Healthy Relationship with Food.* Oakland, CA: New Harbinger Publications Inc., 2017.

UNC School of Medicine. "Survey Finds Disordered Eating Behaviors Among Three Out of Four American Women." *UNC News.* April 22, 2008. Accessed September 6, 2018. www.med.unc.edu/www/newsarchive/2008/april/survey -finds-disordered-eating-behaviors-among-three-out-of-four-american -women.

Vadiveloo, Maya, and Josiemer Mattei. "Perceived Weight Discrimination and 10-Year Risk of Allostatic Load Among US Adults."*Annals of Behavioral Medicine* 51, no. 1 (February 2017): 94–104. doi:10.1007/s12160-016-9831-7.

Vivyan, Carol. "Thought Record Sheet—7 Column." Getselfhelp.co.uk. Accessed September 6, 2018. www.getselfhelp.co.uk/docs/ThoughtRecordSheet7.pdf

Wansink, Brian. *Mindless Eating: Why We Eat More Than We Think.* New York, NY: Bantam, 2006.

Zhou, Linghong, and Jane A. Foster. "Psychobiotics and the Gut-Brain Axis: In the Pursuit of Happiness." *Neuropsychiatric Disease and Treatment* 11 (2015): 715–23. doi:10.2147/NDT.S61997.

INDEX

ACKNOWLEDGMENTS

Thank you to Nana K. Twumasi, Elizabeth Castoria, Carol Rosenberg, and the rest of the team at Althea Press and Callisto Media for helping me take a long-forgotten childhood dream of becoming an author and bring it to life. You make me look and sound better than I ever could.

Thank you to my husband, Brian, for putting up with me when I'm in the depths of my negative self-talk and for making me nourishing meals that taste as good as they look on Instagram.

Thank you to the HAES, fat activist, non-diet, anti-diet, weight-inclusive, and body-positive communities. I'm a relative newbie, and I was embraced with open arms to learn and unlearn together in a brave space.

Thank you to Kate Mak, Casey Berglund, and all the other yoga instructors I've had along the way, for bringing me to mindfulness through the practice of yoga.

Thank you to my family, for giving me life and unconditional support, even if it's from a distance.

Thank you to my patients and clients, who have trusted me with their stories and struggles. You have no idea how much I learn from you, and I am forever grateful.

ABOUT THE AUTHOR

Vincci Tsui is a former bariatric dietitian turned Certified Intuitive Eating Counselor and Health At Every Size advocate. She helps people who are tired of micromanaging their nutrition and health find freedom in their relationship with food and with their body and is passionate about providing and advocating for inclusive care for all.

Born in Hong Kong and raised in Calgary, Vincci received her Bachelor of Science in nutritional sciences from McGill University, and completed the school's integrated dietetic internship. Now back in Calgary, she is a proud member of Dietitians of Canada and the College of Dietitians of Alberta. She is currently pursuing her 200-hour yoga teacher training.

CPSIA information can be obtained
at www.ICGtesting.com
Printed in the USA
LVHW020238050119
602788LV00003B/3/P